The Original Source Code

A Framework for Understanding Humanity, Corruption, and Restoration

Dr. Cassius V. Stuart

You were not designed to function without the Source — you were designed to run on it.

The Original Source Code: A Framework for Understanding Humanity, Corruption, and Restoration

Published by Blue Horizon Books, Plantation, Florida

Nassau, The Bahamas

First edition, 2026. Printed worldwide.

ISBN 979-8-9958941-1-7

Names: Stuart, Cassius V., author.

Title: *The Original Source Code: A Framework for Understanding Humanity, Corruption, and Restoration* / Cassius V. Stuart.

Description: First edition. | Nassau, Bahamas : Blue Horizon Books, 2026. | Includes bibliographical references and index.

Identifiers: ISBN 979-8-9958941-1-7. Subjects:

LCSH: Spiritual life—Christianity. | Human nature—Religious aspects—Christianity. | Sin—Biblical teaching. | Salvation—Christianity. | Theology, Doctrinal.

Classification: LCC BT701 .S78 2026 | DDC 234

The views expressed in this book are those of the author. This work is intended to provide general information on the subject matter covered. It is sold with the understanding that neither the author nor the publisher is engaged in rendering professional, theological, or pastoral services. If such counsel is required, the services of a qualified professional or spiritual advisor should be sought.

Proprietary Framework Notice

The conceptual framework presented in *The Original Source Code*—including the use of system architecture, source code, and transmission models to explain spiritual realities—is an original work developed by the author. These ideas may be cited and discussed for academic, educational, or ministry purposes with proper attribution. No portion may be replicated for commercial use without written permission.

Neither the author nor the publisher shall be liable for any loss, damage, or risk—personal, spiritual, or otherwise—arising from the use of or reliance on the information contained in this book.

Dedication

*To the **One** who bent low over the dust and breathed, and to every soul still listening for that same breath.*

To my family — whose love, patience, and prayers have been the quiet scaffolding beneath every page of this book; whose hours, given up to these chapters, were a gift I did not take for granted.

To every reader who has ever sensed, somewhere underneath the noise of ordinary life, that something in humanity is out of alignment — may you find here both the honest diagnosis and the greater hope.

And, finally, to the Lord Jesus Christ — the Perfect Code, the Second Adam, the radiance of the Father — who did not abandon a corrupted race, but became one of us to restore what was lost.

Soli Deo Gloria.

Contents

SYSTEM MAP / READING PATH

Preface

Something Isn't Running Right

Something isn't right.

You feel it. Not always loudly. Not always clearly. But consistently.

There is a signal beneath the noise of daily life — a low, persistent frequency that tells you the world you are living in, and the person you are living as, are not quite what they were meant to be. It is a signal most people learn to ignore. We silence it with achievement. We bury it under routine. We distract ourselves with pleasures, projects, and performances. And yet the signal does not stop. It only grows quieter, waiting to be heard.

You can succeed and still feel empty. You can know better and still do worse. You can build a life and still feel disconnected from it. You can gather every external marker of a full existence — the title, the income, the relationships, the reputation — and still go to sleep at night with a hollow place inside that none of it has touched.

No matter how much you improve, something underneath remains unresolved. And the reason that is so is not a flaw in you personally. It is the subject of this book.

We Have Been Solving the Wrong Problem

Most people believe the issue is discipline. Or environment. Or knowledge. Or opportunity. So we try to fix ourselves with the tools those assumptions hand us: better habits, better routines, better strategies. We read, we plan, we optimize. We track our sleep. We rewrite our schedules. We join the gym, the program, the mastermind, the church. For a while, it works. We feel momentum. We feel alive. And then, almost imperceptibly, the old patterns return — the irritability, the drift, the inner contradiction, the sense of running hard without arriving anywhere.

Why? Because what we are trying to fix is not what is actually broken. You cannot repair a corrupted program by giving it a faster processor. You cannot resolve a software conflict by replacing the keyboard. You cannot heal a wound by painting over it. And you cannot restore a human being by adjusting the surface while leaving the source untouched.

This Book Makes a Different Claim

This book does not start with behavior. It starts deeper. What if the problem is not what you do — but what you are running on?

What if your thoughts are being influenced by something deeper than thoughts? What if your desires are being shaped at a level you cannot see? What if your sense of identity is not something you created from scratch, but something that was altered — long before you had the capacity to say yes or no to its alteration?

If that is true, then no amount of strategy on the surface will ever reach the issue. The issue is in the code.

The Framework You Are About to Enter

This book introduces a simple but profound idea. You are not merely a person. You are a system. Your body is hardware. Your mind and heart are the operating system. Your life is the output. And at the core of it all — beneath thought, beneath emotion, beneath personality, beneath the habits that seem to run you — is something most people have never seriously considered.

Your source code.

Scripture uses another word for it: spirit. The source layer of a human being is the spirit, and the spirit was designed to operate in direct connection with the Spirit of God. That is not metaphor. That is architecture.

The claim of this book is that in the beginning, God breathed into the dust of man and something far more than biology happened. A code was installed. A signal was activated. A design came online. Humanity did not simply become alive in the biological sense — humanity became a functioning system, animated by the very breath of its Maker.

And the claim of this book is also that, at some point in the earliest history recorded in the Bible, a second kind of input entered that system. Not a minor update. Not a surface scratch. A foreign instruction set — a virus, in the language of our metaphor — that did not erase the original code, but corrupted it. Distorted it. Caused it to run, but no longer to run as designed.

Everything you are experiencing in this life — every inner contradiction, every inconsistency, every success that does not satisfy, every relationship that does not quite connect, every peace that does not last — is the output of a system still running, but running on compromised code.

The Problem Beneath the Surface

You are functioning. But you are not functioning as designed. And that one sentence explains more than a thousand self-help books ever will.

It explains the internal conflict — the person you know you should be quarreling with the person you actually are. It explains the inconsistency — the inability to sustain even the habits you most deeply want. It explains the emptiness success cannot fix — because success was never the missing variable. It explains the universality of the struggle — the fact that this is not happening to you in isolation, but to every human being, in every culture, in every century, throughout recorded history.

This is not random. It is not accidental. It is not personal failure. It is the result of something that happened at the very beginning.

And More Importantly, It Can Be Restored

This book is not just about identifying the problem. It is about understanding where the corruption began, how it continues, why nothing external has fixed it, and — most importantly — how the original design can be restored.

This is the good news hidden in the architecture. A system that was designed can be redesigned. A code that was corrupted can be rewritten. A breath that was given can be given again. And Scripture, from Genesis to Revelation, is the story of exactly that: a Creator refusing to abandon the system He made, patiently moving a fallen creation back toward the alignment it was built for.

A Warning Before You Continue

If you are looking for quick fixes, surface-level advice, or motivation without transformation, this is not that book. This book will challenge how you see yourself, how you understand life, and what you believe the real problem is. It will not always be comfortable. Deep diagnostics rarely are.

But if you are ready to go deeper than behavior—if you are ready to confront the root, stop patching the system, and finally understand the code—then continue reading. Because everything you are experiencing has an origin, has a pattern, has a source. And once you understand the Source, you can finally begin to understand yourself.

Acknowledgments

No book of this kind is written alone. Every page reflects the hands, prayers, and voices of people whose fingerprints I hope the reader will, in some way, be able to feel.

First and above all, I give thanks to God — the Source of life, breath, and restoration. Whatever is true and useful in these pages is borrowed from Him; whatever falls short is mine. This project began as a thought in the middle of the night, and it would never have become a book without the quiet faithfulness of the One who first breathed into dust and who has not stopped breathing into me.

To my wife and children — thank you. You have been patient with the long evenings, the unfinished conversations, and the hours that were owed to you but given instead to these chapters. Every writer who has ever finished a book has done so at the expense of the people who love him most. I am deeply aware that this book exists because of you, not in spite of you, and I could not have done it without your grace.

To the pastors, teachers, mentors, and friends whose sermons, conversations, and examples have shaped the way I read Scripture — thank you. Many of the ideas in this book are not original to me; they are the harvest of years of being discipled by people who loved the Word and loved me enough to share it. I have not always remembered where I first heard something that became foundational; I only know I have been the recipient of a long tradition of faithful teaching, and I hope this book is worthy of the inheritance.

To the readers who have walked with me through earlier projects — especially those who read Success, The Total Package and wrote to tell me what it meant for their lives — thank you for your encouragement and for the many honest questions that sent me back to Scripture to dig deeper. Those questions are woven into the bones of this book.

To the friends who read drafts of these chapters and told me when a sentence was soaring and when it was overreaching — thank you for your time, your theological honesty, and your willingness to disagree with me gently when it mattered. You made this better than it would have been.

To the saints, both living and departed, especially to the late Dr. Myles Munroe and Dr. Richard Pinder, whose lives demonstrated what restored code looks like in practice — teachers, missionaries, mothers, fathers, ordinary believers whose names the world never wrote down — thank you. You are the reason I dared to write a book about restoration in the first place. You showed me it was possible.

And finally, to every reader who has opened this book: thank you for trusting me with a few hours of your life. My prayer is that you will close this book closer to the Source than you were when you opened it — not because my words were clever, but because the breath of the One who spoke at the beginning is still moving, still restoring, still rewriting lives in our own time.

Cassius Stuart

Introduction

The Divine Blueprint

Everyone you've encountered this year—this month, even this week—is carrying corrupted code... a silent virus shaping how they think, act, and live. But it wasn't always this way. Before dysfunction, there was design. Before confusion, there was clarity—an answer written into the architecture itself.

To understand this book, we must begin where the Bible begins — not with man, but with the One who made man. Genesis opens with a Creator acting with intentionality. He does not stumble into the universe. He does not experiment with matter to see what happens. He speaks, and what He speaks comes into being. He separates, He names, He orders, He fills. The opening chapters of Scripture read like the specification document of an engineer: every element placed with purpose, every layer functioning as a precondition for the next.

> *"In the beginning God created the heavens and the earth."*

– Genesis 1:1 (NIV)

The Hebrew verb translated created is bara. Throughout the Hebrew Bible, this verb is used almost exclusively with God as its subject. It describes a kind of making that only God performs — not assembly from pre-existing materials, but the bringing forth of something that was not, into something that now is. This single verb carries a weight of significance that is easy to miss in English translation: the universe is not a found object. It is an intended one.

Life as a Designed System

Every functioning system in the world — biological, mechanical, digital — shares a common structure. It has components. It has interactions among those components. It has a set of rules that govern those interactions. And it has a purpose — an intended outcome that defines what "working correctly" even means. Without purpose, there is no way to distinguish function from malfunction; a clock that keeps any time at all is only a broken clock if we already believe it was meant to keep accurate time.

When Scripture tells us that God created humanity, it is not simply telling us that our species emerged. It is telling us that we were designed. And a designed thing, by definition, carries a standard of working correctly that is not self-chosen, but inscribed by its Designer.

This is the first idea that must be recovered before anything else in this book can make sense: you are a system, and your system has a design, and that design was not written by you.

Humanity as More Than Biology

Modern thinking tends to treat human beings as biological machines — complex ones, certainly, but machines nonetheless. We are presented as collections of tissues, firing neurons, chemical feedback loops, and inherited traits. There is a truth inside this picture. The body is real. The chemistry is real. The biology is not to be dismissed.

But the biblical picture is larger. The Bible does not deny the hardware; it insists there is more than hardware. Human beings in Scripture are never reducible to their matter. There is something else in us — a layer that biology can describe but cannot explain away. That layer is what Scripture calls the spirit, and it is the layer through which a human being is connected to the One who made him.

> *"But it is the spirit in a person, the breath of the Almighty, that gives them understanding."*
>
> **– Job 32:8 (NIV)**

Read that slowly. Understanding does not come from the brain in isolation. Understanding comes from the spirit in a person, and that spirit is identified with the breath of the Almighty. In the biblical framework, human cognition — at its deepest, most meaningful level — is not a purely mechanical process. It is a function of a spirit that was breathed into being by the Spirit of God.

The Moment of Activation

Genesis records the creation of humanity in two distinct motions. First, formation. Then, activation.

> *"Then the LORD God formed a man from the dust of the ground and breathed into his nostrils the breath of life, and the man became a living being."*
>
> **– Genesis 2:7 (NIV)**

The Hebrew verb for formed is yatsar, the verb used for a potter shaping clay. It is artisan language. The first human is not mass-produced. He is crafted, shaped by the fingers of God out of the raw material of the earth. At this point, the hardware exists. The physical structure is in place. Every organ, every system, every cell is present. But he is not yet alive. The form is complete, but the function has not yet begun.

Then God does something that changes everything. He breathes. Into the nostrils of the shaped dust, He exhales what the Hebrew calls the nishmat chayyim — the breath of lives (the noun is plural, suggesting fullness, abundance). And the man becomes a nephesh chayyah — a living soul, a living being.

The form existed before the breath. But the life did not. The design was in place before the activation. But the operation did not begin until the Source breathed.

Breath as the Original Source Code

This is the moment around which this entire book is written. The breath of God into the dust of man is the Original Source Code. Consider what the breath of God accomplishes in that verse. It does not add a body; the body was already shaped. It does not add knowledge; Adam has no memories yet. It does not add strength; Adam will be tested by the weight of his own choices in short order. What the breath adds is life — and with life, everything that makes life human: consciousness, relationship, identity, purpose, moral agency, the capacity to know and be known by God.

In the metaphor of this book, the body is hardware. The mind and heart together form the operating system — the layer that processes input, generates thought, and directs decision. But hardware and operating system together cannot produce a human being. Without the breath, the hardware is only anatomy. Without the breath, the operating system has no power and nothing to run on. What makes the human a human, rather than a highly organized chemical system, is the breath — the source-layer input from God Himself.

Job, centuries later, understood this.

> *"The Spirit of God has made me; the breath of the Almighty gives me life."*
>
> **– Job 33:4 (NIV)**

The Hebrew word for breath in Genesis 2:7 is neshamah. The Hebrew word for Spirit in Job 33:4 is ruach. These two words often overlap in the Hebrew Bible, both carrying the sense of breath, wind, and animating presence. In Greek, the equivalent word is pneuma—the same word translated both as Spirit and as breath in the New Testament. Breath, in biblical thought, is never only biological. Breath is the sign of spirit. And spirit is the sign of life that has come from God.

Why Everything Depends on the Source

If all of this is true — if the defining feature of a human being is not the hardware or the software but the source-layer breath of the Creator — then everything in human experience depends on the continuing relationship of the system to its Source. Cut the connection and the outputs begin to drift. Sever the breath, and the body returns to what it was before the breath entered: dust, waiting to return to the ground.

> *"When you hide your face, they are terrified; when you take away their breath, they die and return to the dust. When you send your Spirit, they are created, and you renew the face of the ground."*
>
> **– Psalm 104:29-30 (NIV)**

Notice the verbs. God sends His Spirit, and life is created. God withdraws His breath, and life ends. The Source is not a one-time starter that the system can operate independently of afterwards. The Source is the ongoing condition of the system. As long as a human being is alive, it is because breath, in the theological sense, is continuing to be given. If a human being is operating correctly, it is because breath, in the deeper sense — the Spirit of God engaging the spirit of man — is continuing to flow.

This is the divine blueprint. And it will be the foundation of everything that follows. Before the breach, before the inherited corruption, before the law, before the promise, before the rebirth, before the restoration, before the Kingdom — there was this. A Designer. A design. A breath. A system activated at the source.

Keep that picture in your mind as you turn the page. Because everything that has gone wrong in the human story is, in the end, a deviation from that first moment. And everything God has done in the long arc of Scripture has been aimed at returning humanity to that moment — and beyond it — to a life fully and permanently running on the original Source Code.

CHAPTER 01

/ THE BUILD

The Build

Divine Architecture

Before there was confusion, there was clarity. Before there was distortion, there was design. And before the breath of God ever filled the nostrils of the first man, there was an architecture — a deliberate, layered, purposeful structure in which that breath was meant to operate.

Humanity did not begin as an accident. It did not begin as a biological experiment. It did not evolve its way into significance after a long and uncertain journey through the nothing. Humanity began as intentional architecture — a system carefully constructed, layered with purpose, and activated with precision. To understand what has gone wrong, we must first understand what was right. To diagnose a corrupted system, you must know what it was supposed to look like when it was working.

Genesis describes the creation of the first human being in two distinct movements: formation and activation. We touched on this briefly in the introduction. In this chapter, we slow down and examine it carefully, because almost everything in this book flows out of the architecture revealed in those two movements.

Formation: The Building of the Hardware

> *"Then the LORD God formed a man from the dust of the ground..."*
>
> – Genesis 2:7a (NIV)

The first movement in the creation of man is formation. The Hebrew verb is yatsar — a verb that describes the work of a potter at his wheel. It is not a word of mass production. It is not the language of an assembly line. It is artisan language. The first human is not stamped out of a mold. He is shaped — carefully, patiently, by the hand of the Creator Himself.

Notice the material. Dust. Afar, in Hebrew. The lowliest, most common substance of the earth. Nothing rare. Nothing precious. Nothing about the raw material that would explain what the dust is about to become. And that is precisely the point. The glory of the human being is not in the material of which he is made, but in the One who shapes him and the breath He places in him.

This is the body. The hardware. The physical structure. The vessel through which the living person will interface with the world. Think of the dust as the substrate — the raw material upon which the Original Source Code would soon be installed. Every organ in it is organized. Every cell is positioned. Every system — circulatory, respiratory, nervous, endocrine — is present and complete. The specification is finished. The device is built.

But at this point, it is still dust. Highly organized dust. Beautifully shaped dust. But dust, nonetheless. It has capacity, but no function. It has structure, but no life. It has the potential for thought, for movement, for speech, for relationship — but not one of those potentials is yet active. The hardware exists, but nothing is running on it.

Activation: The Installation of the Source

> *"...and breathed into his nostrils the breath of life, and the man became a living being."*
>
> **– Genesis 2:7b (NIV)**

The second movement is activation. God bends down to the shaped dust, and He breathes into it. The Hebrew is deeply intimate: vayyippach b'appav nishmat chayyim — He blew into his nostrils the breath of lives. It is the closest physical picture in Scripture of God coming down to the level of His creation. Face to face. Mouth to nostril. Breath to dust.

This is not poetic filler. This is system activation. This is the moment at which the hardware comes online — not because a switch has been flipped, but because the Source has delivered the code that only the Source can deliver.

Before the breath, the body had design without execution. After the breath, the body has life. That single breath is what we will call, throughout this book, the Original Source Code. The word source is important. This is not a first command among many. This is not a stored program sitting somewhere inside the clay waiting to be run.

This is a living transmission from God Himself — an ongoing connection between the Creator and the creature, an animating presence that cannot be separated from its source without the creature ceasing to be what it was designed to be.

The Three-Layer Design of Humanity

From Genesis forward, Scripture consistently describes a human being in terms that correspond to three layers. Different writers emphasize them differently. The Apostle Paul, in a particularly clear moment, prays for all three explicitly:

> *"May God himself, the God of peace, sanctify you through and through. May your whole spirit, soul and body be kept blameless at the coming of our Lord Jesus Christ."*

– 1 Thessalonians 5:23 (NIV)

Spirit. Soul. Body. Three distinct layers, woven into one integrated system. Some theologians have debated whether these are three separable parts or three facets of a single person. For our purposes, the debate is less important than the recognition that Scripture consistently distinguishes between these three aspects and that each has a role to play in the functioning of the whole. Using the systems language of this book, we can translate the three layers this way.

1. The Body — Hardware

The body is the physical vessel. It is the interface through which the human person receives input from the world and delivers output to the world. Eyes, ears, hands, voice, posture, nervous system – all of it is hardware. Without source-layer code, hardware is only matter; it sits, inert, waiting. Given source-layer code, hardware becomes expression. Through the body, thoughts become words, intentions become actions, inner alignment becomes visible presence in the world. The body matters in Scripture. It is not a prison from which to escape. It is a vessel to be honored and, ultimately, redeemed.

2. The Mind and Heart — Operating System

The mind and heart together form the operating system of the human being. The mind processes input – perception, thought, reasoning. The heart, in biblical usage, is not merely the seat of emotion but the center of desire, motivation, allegiance, and will. Proverbs tells us:

> *"Above all else, guard your heart, for everything you do flows from it."*
>
> **– Proverbs 4:23 (NIV)**

Everything you do flows from the heart. That is operating-system language. The heart is where deep decisions are made, where values are weighted, where the pull of this or that possibility is registered. Together with the mind, it determines how inputs from the world are translated into outputs through the body.

3. The Spirit — Source Code

Beneath the body and beneath the mind and heart, there is a deeper layer still. Scripture calls it the spirit. In Hebrew, ruach. In Greek, pneuma. The same words used for breath and for wind, reflecting an animating presence that is real but not material. This is the deepest layer of a human being. It is the governing layer — the level at which connection to God happens, at which identity and purpose are defined, at which the whole system is either aligned to its Source or misaligned from it.

The spirit is not an accessory to human life. It is not an optional extra for the religiously inclined. In the biblical framework, the spirit is the core instruction set from which everything else flows. When the spirit is functioning properly—when it is in living connection with the Spirit of God—the operating system runs cleanly and the body executes well. When the spirit is disconnected or corrupted, the whole system drifts, and every other layer begins to express that drift.

Designed to Run on Source

From the beginning, humanity was not designed to function independently. This is a claim so foreign to modern thinking that it bears repeating: humanity was not designed to function independently.

Man was not built to generate his own meaning. He was not built to define his own truth. He was not built to construct his own purpose out of personal preference and social approval. All of those things were already embedded in the Source. Identity was given. Purpose was assigned. Authority was established. Connection to God was direct.

There was no confusion in the original system, because there was no separation from the Source. The system was fully aligned.

> *"So God created mankind in his own image, in the image of God he created them; male and female he created them."*
>
> **– Genesis 1:27 (NIV)**

The phrase image of God — tselem Elohim in Hebrew — is one of the most dense phrases in all of Scripture. It does not mean that God has a body like ours. It means that the human being was designed to reflect, in limited but real ways, the character and nature of the God who made him. Relational. Creative. Moral. Purposeful. Able to love. Able to choose. Able to know and be known. The image is not a decoration; it is a functional description of what the human system was built to display.

Perfect Alignment

In this original state, there was no internal conflict. The mind did not war against the spirit. The heart did not distort truth. The body did not act against its design. Everything flowed from the Source. There was no need for correction, because there was no error. There was no need for law, because there was no deviation. There was no need for effort, because alignment was natural.

This is critical. Humanity did not start broken. Humanity started whole. This is one of the most important claims in the entire biblical worldview, and it sets this framework apart from almost every competing account of the human condition. In many ancient mythologies, humans are accidents, afterthoughts, or intentional slaves to the gods. In modern secular frameworks, humans are the outcome of a purposeless evolutionary process that produced a creature capable of suffering far beyond its capacity to find meaning. In the biblical story, humans are neither of those things. Humans began whole, intact, in alignment, in communion, without inner contradiction, without fear, without shame, without fracture.

If you begin at any other place, you will end at any other place. If you assume humanity was always broken, then brokenness is just part of what it means to be human, and the best you can hope for is management. But if humanity was once whole, then wholeness is not a fantasy. It is a memory. And it is a destination.

Identity Before Performance

One of the greatest misunderstandings in the modern world is the belief that people must perform their way into identity. We are told, from childhood, that we will become somebody once we achieve, accomplish, and accumulate. Our identity is presented as a reward at the end of a long performance, always receding as we draw near.

But in the original design, identity came first. Adam did not earn his worth. He did not prove his value. He did not discover his purpose through trial and error. All of it was already written into the code. He was, by virtue of being made in the image of God, a being of immense worth before he lifted a finger. He was, by virtue of being breathed into by God, alive with purpose before he named a single animal.

This is what it means to be created in the image of God—not merely resemblance, but reflection of divine intention. The human person is not an argument that has to be won. The human person is a gift that has already been given. Everything that comes afterward—work, dominion, relationship, culture—is the expression of identity, not the earning of it.

> *"For you created my inmost being; you knit me together in my mother's womb. I praise you because I am fearfully and wonderfully made; your works are wonderful, I know that full well."*

– Psalm 139:13-14 (NIV)

The psalmist is not describing himself as an accident who has achieved importance. He is describing himself as a designed being, recognized by his Designer before he ever lifted a hand or spoke a word. This is identity before performance.

Dominion: Authority in the System

Part of the original code included dominion.

> *"God blessed them and said to them, 'Be fruitful and increase in number; fill the earth and subdue it. Rule over the fish in the sea and the birds in the sky and over every living creature that moves on the ground.'"*
>
> **– Genesis 1:28 (NIV)**

Man was not placed in creation as a passive observer. He was given authority — to steward, to lead, to govern under God. The Hebrew verb radah, translated rule, carries the sense of exercising responsible authority on behalf of another. Adam was not made to be a king independent of his Maker. He was made to be a viceroy — a ruler deriving his authority from the true King and answerable to Him.

This distinction matters enormously. In the original code, human authority was not independent. It was derived. As long as man remained connected to the Source, his authority functioned properly. It was aligned. It was measured. It was purposeful. It had boundaries within which it could safely and beautifully operate.

Remove the Source, and authority becomes distorted. A branch can only bear fruit while it remains connected to the vine; a branch cut off does not suddenly flower on the strength of its own wood. In exactly the same way, a human being cannot exercise authority rightly once the connection to God has been severed. Derived authority, untethered from its source, becomes either tyranny or paralysis.

The System Before the Breach

Before the fall, the system operated with clarity, peace, connection, and integrity. **Clarity** — there was no confusion about identity or purpose. **Peace** — there was no internal fragmentation. **Connection** — there was direct communion with God. **Integrity** — there was no contradiction between design and function.

Nothing was missing. Nothing was broken. Nothing needed to be fixed. Adam walked with God in the cool of the day. He named the animals. He received a wife made of his own substance and recognized her immediately as bone of his bone and flesh of his flesh. He lived in a garden specifically prepared for his flourishing. He had meaningful work to do. He had boundaries to honor. He had a relationship that was closer than we can imagine with the God whose breath still moved inside him.

Why This Matters

If you misunderstand the original design, you will misdiagnose the problem. If you assume humanity started flawed, you will accept dysfunction as normal. You will treat every symptom as natural rather than acquired. You will medicate rather than restore. You will resign yourself to a version of yourself you were never meant to live with.

If you think the issue is behavior, you will try to fix actions instead of addressing the source. You will exhaust yourself optimizing habits that keep collapsing. You will rotate through self-help systems, looking for the one that finally sticks. And it will not stick, because the issue was never at the layer your systems are operating on.

If you ignore the code, you will keep patching the system — and wondering why it keeps failing. You will fix a leak in one place and find another leak opening up somewhere else. You will solve the crisis of this year only to find the crisis of next year is the same crisis wearing a different face. Nothing is wrong with you as a patcher; the problem is that the code itself needs to be addressed, and patches are not written in the code's language. But once you understand the first truth — that the system was built perfectly — you begin to ask the right question. Not "Why am I like this?" but "What altered the code?"

The Tension We Live In

Every human being, whether they realize it or not, carries within them a quiet sense that something is off. There is a gap between who we are and who we feel we should be. There is a disconnect between success and satisfaction. There is a constant search for something we cannot fully define.

Saint Augustine, in the fourth century, put it this way in the opening paragraph of his Confessions: "You have made us for Yourself, O Lord, and our heart is restless until it rests in You." That restlessness is not a pathology. It is evidence. It is the echo of the original architecture — a residual signal from the design, insisting that the system was meant for something more. That tension does not come from poor design. It comes from deviation from the design.

Closing Thought

You were never meant to figure life out on your own. You were designed to run on the Source. The Three-Layer Design — body as hardware, mind and heart as operating system, spirit as source code — was never meant to function as a self-contained unit. It was designed for connection. And until you understand the architecture — body, operating system, source code; dust, breath, and the God who bent down to blow into it — you will keep trying to fix a system without ever touching the code.

The Bible is, at its deepest level, a book about the architecture of what you are and the history of what has happened to that architecture. It is not a collection of moral advice. It is not a self-improvement manual. It is a design document, a damage report, and a restoration plan — and until you read it in that key, the whole thing will sound like a scattered anthology. Read in that key, it becomes a single, relentless story, sweeping from the first breath in Genesis to the final breath of heaven in Revelation, telling the story of the original Source Code, what happened to it, and what the Source Himself has done to get it running again.

CHAPTER 02

/ THE BREATH

The Breath

Code Activation

Of all the moments in Scripture, few carry more weight than the moment the breath of God entered the body of man. It is a moment so familiar to readers of the Bible that its strangeness often gets lost. But if you were encountering this story for the first time, you would not be able to read past it without stopping. The God who has spoken the universe into existence — who has only had to say "let there be" for stars and seas and creatures to appear — pauses, bends down, and exhales into a shaped piece of earth. Speech was enough for everything else. For man, the Creator uses breath.

In the language of this book, that is the moment the original Source Code was installed.

> *"Then the LORD God formed a man from the dust of the ground and breathed into his nostrils the breath of life, and the man became a living being."*
>
> **– Genesis 2:7 (NIV)**

The Breath of Life as Divine Input

The Hebrew phrase translated breath of life is ***nishmat chayyim***. Nishmat derives from neshamah, a word that refers specifically to the breath of a living being — deeper than the simple air moving in and out, it carries the sense of the vital force itself, the signal of life. ***Chayyim*** is the plural form of chay, life. Literally: the breath of lives.

Why plural? Hebrew uses plurals in several ways, including what grammarians call the plural of abundance — a plural form used to emphasize fullness, completeness, intensity. Elohim, the common Hebrew word for God, is a grammatically plural form used with singular verbs; it implies not multiple gods but a fullness of deity beyond anything singular language can contain. Chayyim functions similarly here. God did not blow a narrow biological breath into man. He blew the fullness of life every dimension of what it means to be alive: biological life, mental life, emotional life, relational life, spiritual life, moral life, purposeful life. All of it was contained in that breath.

This is important because in our modern context, we tend to hear the word life in very narrow terms. Life is what a heart monitor measures. Life is the presence of a pulse. Life is the absence of death. But in Hebrew thought, life is much more than that. Life is relational. Life is moral. Life is purposeful. Life is communion. A body can have a pulse and not be alive in the deeper sense; a dead man walking through his days, going through the motions, is a figure Scripture will return to again and again.

> *"As for you, you were dead in your transgressions and sins."*
>
> **– Ephesians 2:1 (NIV)**

Paul is not describing corpses. He is describing people who appear by every biological measure to be alive, but who have lost connection to the source of real life. Their hardware is running. Their operating systems are processing. But the source-layer connection is severed, and therefore the fullness of what life was meant to be is absent. This is what Paul means by dead in trespasses.

Genesis 2:7 is the opposite. Adam is not just biologically animated. He is alive with chayyim. He is alive at every layer at once, because the breath of God has activated every layer at once.

The Difference Between Existing and Being Alive

This leads to one of the most important distinctions in Scripture: the difference between existing and being alive.

Rocks exist. Water exists. Planets exist. By virtue of the act of creation, matter is. But existence is not the same thing as life. A rock is not alive. A lake is not alive. Existence is the baseline; life is something more.

Plants have a kind of life. They grow, reproduce, respond to stimuli. Animals have a deeper kind of life. They move, sense, form social patterns. But the human being, in the biblical account, has a life that exceeds both plant and animal life by an order of magnitude. And the explanation is not in the hardware. The explanation is in the breath. God did not breathe into the fish. He did not breathe into the sparrow. He did not breathe into the trees of the garden. He breathed into the one creature He had shaped with His own hands, and that breath is why the human is unlike anything else in the created order.

To exist is to take up space. To be alive, in the full biblical sense, is to take up relationship — relationship with God, with other human beings, with creation itself, and with one's own inner life. The breath of God into man made all of that possible. Without the breath, Adam might have existed in some sense. With the breath, he could live.

Full Alignment with the Creator

At the moment of activation, the human system was in full alignment with its Creator. There was no gap. There was no hesitation. There was no distortion between what God intended and what the man experienced. The code had just been installed, and it was running without error.

What does full alignment look like? Consider what Adam's immediate experience must have been. He is conscious of himself. He is conscious of his environment. He is conscious of God's presence. But he has no inner accuser, no hidden shame, no private fear. His thoughts agree with his feelings, which agree with his desires, which agree with his actions. The three layers — body, mind and heart, spirit — are not only all present; they are all pointing in the same direction.

The Apostle James, many centuries later, described the corrupted state we now know as double-minded — dipsuchos in Greek, literally two-souled.

> *"Such a person is double-minded and unstable in all they do."*
>
> **– James 1:8 (NIV)**

Adam in Genesis 2 is the opposite of double-minded. He is single-souled. His whole being bends in one direction. His whole system runs in one key. When God speaks, the words land without resistance. When God gives instruction, the instruction is received as trustworthy, not negotiated against internally. There is no second voice yet, whispering alternative interpretations. The signal from the Source is clean, and the system is receiving it cleanly.

This is the state in which human beings were originally intended to operate. Not perfect in the sense of having done everything possible; perfect in the sense of being without contradiction. Whole. Integrated. Aligned. Clean.

Original Harmony: No Conflict, No Fragmentation

In the opening chapters of Genesis, there is a remarkable repeated phrase. After nearly every act of creation, God pronounces the result tov — good. Not good in a watered-down, modern sense; good in the sense of functioning as designed, reflecting the wisdom of the Creator, delighting the One who made it. Six times the narrator records God saying it is good. And at the end of the sixth day, after the creation of man and woman in His image, God raises the intensity of the language:

> *"God saw all that he had made, and it was very good."*
>
> **– Genesis 1:31 (NIV)**

Tov me'od — very good. The whole system, at the moment of completion, was operating in harmony. Not only was each part functioning correctly; each part was functioning correctly in relationship to every other part. This is a feature of designed systems: you can have components that are individually fine but that fail when combined because they were not designed to work together. In the original creation, that was not the case. Everything was designed to work together, and at the beginning, everything did.

For Adam, this harmony meant several things simultaneously. It meant no conflict within himself: his body did what his heart desired, his heart desired what his mind knew was right, his mind knew what his spirit perceived from God. It meant no conflict between himself and God: he was not ashamed, not afraid, not hiding. And it meant no conflict between himself and his environment: the ground was not fighting him, the animals were not at war with him, his food was provided, his work was meaningful, his place was clear.

This harmony is not the absence of challenge. Adam was given work to do. The garden had to be tended. The animals had to be named. His wife would eventually be brought to him, and he would receive and love her. Harmony does not mean nothing happens. It means that whatever happens, happens in an environment where the system is not at war with itself.

The Breath That Returns to God

It is worth pausing here to note something that the writer of Ecclesiastes, looking back at the long experience of human life under the sun, wrote many centuries later:

> *"and the dust returns to the ground it came from, and the spirit returns to God who gave it."*
>
> **– Ecclesiastes 12:7 (NIV)**

The breath that was given is a breath that belongs ultimately to God. The spirit of a human being is not self-generated. It was breathed in, and at death it will be breathed back. This is not alarming. It is clarifying. The life that animates a human being is on loan from its Maker. The body is shaped from dust and, absent the breath, returns to dust. The spirit is given by God and, at the moment of death, returns to Him.

We are, to adopt the metaphor once more, always running on source-layer input that is not native to the hardware. We are always running on borrowed breath. This was true from Genesis 2:7 onward, and it has never stopped being true. No one has ever been alive on the strength of his or her own matter.

The Breath and the Image

Only one creature in all of creation is described as being made in the image of God: the human. Only one creature is described as being animated by the direct breath of God into its nostrils: the human. These two descriptions are not separate facts about us. They are two ways of describing the same reality. The image of God is carried in a being who is alive by the breath of God. Remove the breath, and the image has no vessel. Remove the image, and the breath has no subject. The two belong together.

This is why, of all the creatures in the garden, only the human is capable of a certain kind of wreckage. Fish cannot sin. Birds cannot rebel. A lion cannot blaspheme. But a human being, alive by the breath of God and made in His image, has been given the terrible and beautiful capacity to respond — to receive the relationship on offer, or to refuse it; to align to the Source, or to detach from it; to let the breath govern the system, or to try to run the system on some other input. That capacity is itself part of what it means to be made in the image of a free God. And, of course, that capacity is precisely where the rest of this story will begin to turn.

Closing Thought

Before the breach, there was the breath. Before the distortion, there was the activation. Before the long and painful arc of human failure, there was a moment of pure, unobstructed life — a moment of single-souled harmony — a moment when the original Source Code was running cleanly and the system was functioning exactly as designed.

Keep that moment in your mind. Everything that comes next will be, in one way or another, a departure from it or a return to it. The breach in Chapter 3 is a departure. The restoration that begins in Chapter 9 is a return. And the Kingdom in Chapter 15 is a return that has become permanent — a moment of original harmony restored, secured, and made unbreakable forever.

Every time the Bible pictures something new and good happening to a human being, it reaches for this vocabulary. Living water. New birth. Breath of the Spirit. New creation. The language keeps circling back to Genesis 2:7, because the problem the Bible is addressing keeps being a problem at the level of that first breath — and the solution the Bible is offering keeps being, in one form or another, a renewal of that breath.

CHAPTER 03

/ THE BREACH

The Breach

When the System Was Compromised

Every system that fails has a moment where it was first altered. Not always visibly. Not always dramatically. But decisively. Humanity did not drift into dysfunction over time. It crossed a line.

In Genesis 3, that moment is recorded with unsettling simplicity: a conversation, a choice, and a shift that would ripple through every generation that ever followed. If you came to the Bible looking for a long, elaborate account of how the human race was corrupted, you would be disappointed by how short the story actually is. The breach is told in twenty-four verses. No special effects. No cosmic battle. Just a conversation by a tree, a piece of fruit, and two people who will never again be the same.

The brevity is the point. What seems like a small event becomes the inflection point of the entire human story. It is the moment the Source Code was compromised.

The System Was Secure

Before the breach, the system was secure. Fully aligned. Operating exactly as designed. God had given Adam one explicit instruction and a wide, generous permission.

> *"And the LORD God commanded the man, 'You are free to eat from any tree in the garden; but you must not eat from the tree of the knowledge of good and evil, for when you eat from it you will certainly die.'"*
>
> **– Genesis 2:16-17 (NIV)**

Notice the ratio. A whole garden of permission; a single tree of restriction. The boundary is not arbitrary, and it is not oppressive. It is the one place in the entire environment where Adam is asked to acknowledge that he is a creature, not the creator. That he is a subject under authority, not a sovereign of his own making. That he lives by the instruction of God, not by the invention of his own rules. Every other tree is his to enjoy.

The one tree is the system integrity check — the acknowledgment, in practice, that he runs on Source, and not on self. This is an important point. Obedience in the garden was not compliance with a burdensome law. It was the ongoing expression of the creature's trust in its Creator. God's instruction was an invitation to remain in alignment. Disobedience would not be a trivial infraction; it would be the severing of the very alignment that made the system work.

The First Intrusion

Then, into that secure environment, an external voice entered.

> *"Now the serpent was more crafty than any of the wild animals the LORD God had made. He said to the woman, 'Did God really say, "You must not eat from any tree in the garden"?'"*
>
> – **Genesis 3:1 (NIV)**

The serpent does not begin with force. He does not overwhelm. He does not threaten. He begins with a question — and the question is a probe. It is designed to introduce doubt into the operating layer, because if the mind and heart can be altered, the system can be compromised.

Notice the subtle distortion in the question itself. God had said, "You are free to eat from any tree in the garden," with one exception. The serpent reframes the boundary: "Did God really say, 'You must not eat from any tree'?" He inflates the restriction, shrinks the generosity, and misrepresents the character of God — all in a single question. The technique is brilliant, because it is not yet a claim. It is only a question. A question does not yet commit the one asking to a position. But it forces the hearer to consider a position that was not under consideration a moment before.

This is how all malicious code enters a clean system. It does not announce itself as malicious. It arrives as a query, a suggestion, a reasonable-sounding alternative. It asks for permission to be considered, and in the considering, it begins its work.

> *"But I am afraid that just as Eve was deceived by the serpent's cunning, your minds may somehow be led astray from your sincere and pure devotion to Christ."*
>
> **– 2 Corinthians 11:3 (NIV)**

Paul, looking back on Genesis 3, identifies the mechanism: cunning. The attack was not on the body. It was on the mind — the operating system. And Paul warns the Corinthians that the same mechanism is still operational. Nothing about the breach has been made obsolete by the passing of centuries. The serpent's playbook is still in use.

The Progression of the Probe

Watch how the attack deepens. It begins with a question. It moves to a flat contradiction of God's word. It ends with a redefinition of God's motive.

> *"'You will not certainly die,' the serpent said to the woman. 'For God knows that when you eat from it your eyes will be opened, and you will be like God, knowing good and evil.'"*
>
> **– Genesis 3:4-5 (NIV)**

You will not certainly die — a direct contradiction of God's explicit warning. God is portrayed as either dishonest or mistaken. Either way, His word is no longer reliable, and therefore the most basic input in the system — the voice of the

Creator — becomes, in the hearer's assessment, an input to be questioned.

God knows — a pivot to motive. God is now portrayed as self-interested, as withholding something from you that He has secretly been keeping for Himself. The boundary is no longer a gift; it is a restriction imposed by a God who does not want you to rise above your station. The whole framing shifts. What was love is now control. What was protection is now jealousy. What was trust is now suspicion.

You will be like God — a redirection of identity. The serpent offers the one thing humans already possessed, but in a form that requires detachment from the Source to obtain. Adam and Eve were already made in the image of God. They already participated in His life. The offer of the serpent is not a new gift; it is the old gift repackaged as something you must seize by rebellion rather than receive by relationship.

Unauthorized Modification

The instruction from God was clear. The boundary was defined. But disobedience was not just breaking a rule. It was a rewrite of trust. At the moment the fruit was taken and eaten, three things collapsed simultaneously.

Truth was questioned. The serpent's word was weighed against God's word, and the serpent's won. This was not a debate settled by reason; it was a preference settled by desire. The moment desire was given the authority to arbitrate between God's word and another word, a new operating principle had replaced the old. The Source was no longer the final reference.

Authority was challenged. God had said one thing. Adam and Eve did another. The derivation of authority from the Source was broken; in its place, authority was claimed as self-held. They would decide for themselves what was good and what was evil. They would become, in their own minds, the arbiters of reality. But a derived authority cannot survive separation from its source — which meant, in reality, they had not seized authority; they had forfeited it.

Dependence on the Source was replaced with self-determination. The code was rewritten. And with one act of disobedience, the system accepted foreign input.

That is the breach.

What Actually Happened

The body did not collapse. The mind did not shut down. Life continued. Adam did not keel over on the spot. He ate. His wife ate. They looked at each other. The sun kept rising. By any surface measurement, nothing dramatic had occurred. In one sense, the serpent had been right: they did not physically die the instant they bit.

But something deeper had changed. The source layer was altered. Alignment with God was broken. Identity became unstable. The system lost its reference point. The breath of God was still in them. The hardware was still functioning. The operating system was still processing. But something in the deepest layer had been corrupted, and its corruption was about to begin cascading through every other layer.

This is critical: the problem was not that humanity stopped functioning. The problem is that it continued functioning — incorrectly. A system that has stopped is easy to recognize. A system that is still running but running wrong is often not recognized at all. It blends in. It looks normal. It even makes claims about its own normality. And the longer it runs in its corrupted state, the more everyone around it begins to assume that the corrupted state is what was intended all along.

Immediate System Effects

The moment the breach occurred, the symptoms appeared — not after years of accumulating decisions, but instantly, in the same chapter.

> *"Then the eyes of both of them were opened, and they realized they were naked; so they sewed fig leaves together and made coverings for themselves."*

– Genesis 3:7 (NIV)

Awareness without covering. The first effect is a new kind of self-consciousness. They are suddenly aware of their own exposure — not just physically, but morally and existentially. They know they are seen, and they know that being seen is now a problem. They try to manufacture a covering out of what is available. The fig leaves are the first recorded human attempt at self-justification, at performance, at managing the consequences of corruption through external means. It will not be the last.

> *"Then the man and his wife heard the sound of the LORD God as he was walking in the garden in the cool of the day, and they hid from the LORD God among the trees of the garden."*

– Genesis 3:8 (NIV)

Fear replaces peace. The same voice, the same presence, the same walk in the cool of the day — but now it is terror instead of communion. Nothing has changed in God. Everything has changed in them. Peace has been replaced with fear, and the very presence they were designed to thrive in becomes the presence they hide from.

> *"The man said, 'The woman you put here with me—she gave me some fruit from the tree, and I ate it.' Then the LORD God said to the woman, 'What is this you have done?' The woman said, 'The serpent deceived me, and I ate.'"*

– Genesis 3:12-13 (NIV)

Blame replaces responsibility. The man blames the woman — and implicitly, God Himself. The woman blames the serpent. Nowhere in the exchange is a simple confession: "I did this." The system has begun to deflect rather than align. Responsibility, which is a function of clean alignment at the source, has become unbearable, and deflection has become the default.

Separation from the Source. Eventually God drives them from the garden — not out of spite, but as a protective act. To remain in the garden with the tree of life, in a state of corruption, would be to freeze the corruption in place for eternity. Expulsion is mercy. But expulsion is also evidence: the connection that once was direct is now disrupted. Access is no longer automatic. The communion that was assumed has become something that must be sought.

These are not random emotional reactions. They are outputs of corrupted code. They are not failures in and of themselves; they are symptoms of a deeper failure. And they appeared instantly — not because the mechanism of decay is fast, but because the mechanism of alignment is immediate. When the alignment was severed, the effects of severed alignment began at once.

The Nature of the Breach

This was not a surface-level issue. It was not behavior alone. It was not ignorance. It was not a lack of discipline. The problem was not that Adam and Eve had weak willpower or poor impulse control. It was not a training problem. It was a trust problem. A loyalty problem. A source problem.

It was internal corruption at the root level. The system that once received instruction directly from God was now operating on a distorted internal framework. The filter had changed. The reference point had shifted. The question of what is real and what is good was no longer settled by the voice of the Creator. It was being settled by a newly installed internal authority —

the self — that was, in fact, incompetent to settle such questions.

The Illusion of Autonomy

At the heart of the breach was one idea: You can be like God. Not in form — but in function. Independent. Self-defining. Self-governing. And this is where the corruption deepens.

Because humanity did not just disobey. It detached from its Source and attempted to operate on its own authority. It declared independence, not only from a particular command, but from the whole relational architecture in which commands had made sense. It was no longer willing to live as a creature in living connection with a Creator. It wanted to become a kind of lesser creator in its own right — the arbiter of its own reality, the author of its own meaning, the judge of its own actions.

But here is the truth the serpent did not mention: a system designed to run on Source cannot sustain itself without it. The branch can pretend to be a tree. It cannot actually become one. The lamp can pretend it generates its own light. It cannot actually keep shining with the cord pulled. What looks like autonomy in a derived being is always, in reality, a slow drift toward collapse.

> *"My people have committed two sins: They have forsaken me, the spring of living water, and have dug their own cisterns, broken cisterns that cannot hold water."*
>
> **– Jeremiah 2:13 (NIV)**

Forsake the spring. Dig your own cisterns. The cisterns will be broken. The water will leak out. And you will end up thirsty in a landscape you thought you could make yours by declaration. This is the long, sad echo of the breach, still being heard thousands of years later.

Compromised, Not Destroyed

The image of God in humanity was not erased. It was distorted. The system still had capacity, but not clarity. Still had function, but not alignment. This is a subtle but extremely important point.

After Genesis 3, human beings are still the image-bearers of God. They still possess rationality, creativity, moral awareness, relational capacity, and enormous worth. A few chapters later, when Genesis warns against murder, it grounds the warning precisely in the fact that the image of God is still carried in every human being:

> *"Whoever sheds human blood, by humans shall their blood be shed; for in the image of God has God made mankind."*
>
> **– Genesis 9:6 (NIV)**

Post-fall humanity is still in the image of God. But the image is, to borrow a phrase, a cracked mirror. The reflection is still there, but the picture is distorted. Love is possible, but it is now tangled with selfishness. Truth is possible, but it is now tangled with deception. Creativity is possible, but it is now tangled with destruction. Everything the human being was built to do, the human being still can do. But almost nothing is now done cleanly.

This is why humanity is capable of both brilliance and destruction. Love and selfishness. Truth and deception. Stunning art and devastating evil — often from the same person, sometimes in the same day. The code is still there. It is just corrupted.

Why the Breach Matters

If you misunderstand the breach, you will misunderstand everything that follows. You will think people just need better choices. You will believe discipline can fix the issue. You will assume knowledge is the solution, that information is enough, that if people just knew better they would do better. You will reach for every lever except the one that is actually in play.

But none of those address the root problem. Because the issue is not external behavior. It is internal corruption. A person who is perfectly informed and perfectly disciplined and perfectly resourced, but whose source layer is still corrupted, is still a corrupted system. The outputs will still be off. The internal contradictions will still appear. The same tragedy that plays out on the global stage will play out, in quieter forms, in every private life.

The Point of No Return

Once the breach occurred, humanity could not simply "go back." You cannot unmake a decision that altered the system. You cannot reverse corruption through effort. You cannot restore original code from within a compromised system. A virus that has written itself into the registry cannot be undone by the program it has compromised.

Something else would be required. Something outside the system. Someone not bound by the compromise. The rest of the Bible is the long, patient unfolding of what that Someone would have to be, and what He would have to do, to restore a humanity that could not restore itself.

Transition to What Comes Next

The breach did not stay contained. It did not end with Adam and Eve. It multiplied. It spread. It embedded itself into the very process of human existence, so that every child born into the world from that moment forward would inherit not just physical traits, but the corrupted code itself. This is the disturbing claim that will occupy the next chapter: the corruption did not just begin in humanity. It began to reproduce through it.

CHAPTER 04

/ INHERITED CODE

Inherited Code

Born in Sin

The breach did not stay contained. It did not end in a moment. It became a pattern. Then a condition. Then a reality every human is born into.

What began as a single act in Genesis did not remain isolated. It replicated. The choice of one man became the inheritance of every man. The corruption that entered one system began to spread through every system that descended from it. And this is the point at which the biblical account makes one of its most unsettling and most clarifying claims: the problem is not just what people do. The problem is what people are.

From Event to Inheritance

The fall was not just something humanity did. It became something humanity is. From that point forward, every human being enters life not from a neutral state, but from a compromised starting point. Not taught first. Not learned over time. But inherited at the core.

David, writing from the perspective of someone who has just been confronted with the depth of his own sin, articulates this clearly:

> *"Surely I was sinful at birth, sinful from the time my mother conceived me."*
>
> **– Psalm 51:5 (NIV)**

This is not a statement about behavior. It is a statement about nature. David is not claiming that he was delivered into the world doing sinful acts as a newborn; that would be absurd. He is claiming something far deeper. He is claiming that the orientation from which all his sins would flow was already present at the moment of his conception. The corrupted code was not installed by experience; it was inherited in the womb.

Job, in a passage often overlooked, says something similar:

> *"Who can bring what is pure from the impure? No one!"*
>
> **– Job 14:4 (NIV)**

The logic is straightforward. If the source is corrupted, what comes from the source will carry the corruption. You do not get pure water from a poisoned well. You do not get clean code from a compromised repository. And you do not get untainted descendants from a tainted ancestry.

Paul's Diagnosis

The Apostle Paul, more than any other New Testament writer, lays out the logic of inherited corruption with relentless clarity. Writing to the Romans, he says:

> *"Therefore, just as sin entered the world through one man, and death through sin, and in this way death came to all people, because all sinned."*
>
> **– Romans 5:12 (NIV)**

Sin entered through one man. The entry point is identified. The person is named. The vector is specific. Sin did not evolve as a byproduct of social complexity; it entered through one man. And death came through sin — the two are linked. And in this way death came to all people, because all sinned. The past tense is significant. It is not only that all people sin, present tense; it is that all sinned, in Adam, in the one-man moment that became the many-generation inheritance.

A few verses later, Paul is even more explicit about the corporate, inherited nature of what happened:

> *"For just as through the disobedience of the one man the many were made sinners, so also through the obedience of the one man the many will be made righteous."*
>
> **– Romans 5:19 (NIV)**

Were made sinners. This is passive. This is something that was done to us, not something we engineered for ourselves. The sinner condition precedes the sinful act. The orientation precedes the expression. Paul is arguing that humanity stands in solidarity with Adam in a way that is as real and as foundational as its potential to stand in solidarity with Christ. Both realities are structural, not merely individual.

And then later, in the great fifteenth chapter of First Corinthians:

> *"For since death came through a man, the resurrection of the dead comes also through a man. For as in Adam all die, so in Christ all will be made alive."*
>
> **– 1 Corinthians 15:21-22 (NIV)**

In Adam, all die. The inheritance is universal. No culture has been found that escaped it. No civilization has been identified that was somehow exempt. Every human being who has ever lived has lived under the shadow of the Adamic condition, which is not merely a vulnerability to sin but a present orientation toward it.

Procreation as the Replication Mechanism

Human life reproduces through procreation. It is, in the language of this framework, the replication mechanism — the channel through which both life and condition are copied from one generation to the next. What is passed is not only biology. DNA carries physical traits. But something else is carried too — what the Bible calls, in various places, the flesh, the old man, the body of sin. Call it, for our purposes, internal disposition. And that disposition is carried with the life, from parent to child, from generation to generation, without interruption.

Every new life is not just a fresh start. It is a continuation of the existing system. When a baby is born, a new person enters the world — a person with unique traits, potential, personality, gifts. But that new person enters with a default configuration that is not neutral. The factory settings have been altered. The firmware — the deep internal programming that shapes behavior below the level of conscious choice — has been affected before the child draws a first breath.

If the system is corrupted, what is produced will carry that corruption. That is not a judgment on the baby. The baby is not morally responsible for what it has inherited. But the baby is, from day one, running on the same compromised code as every human who has come before.

This is why the problem is universal. Not cultural. Not environmental. Not educational. Universal.

> *"As it is written: 'There is no one righteous, not even one; there is no one who understands; there is no one who seeks God. All have turned away, they have together become worthless; there is no one who does good, not even one.'"*
>
> **– Romans 3:10-12 (NIV)**

Paul is stringing together quotations from the Old Testament — from the Psalms, from Isaiah — and the point of his mosaic is unmistakable. The problem is not a specific ethnic group. Not a particular social class. Not an identifiable set of bad people that could be fenced off from the good people. There is no one righteous. The diagnosis spans the whole species.

Sin Versus Sins: The Critical Distinction

To understand the depth of the issue, we must separate two ideas that the English language tends to blur together.

Sins, plural. Actions. Behaviors. Visible expressions. The lie told. The affair pursued. The anger unleashed. The pride paraded. These are things a person does. They can be counted. They can be confessed. They can be regretted.

Sin, singular. The condition. The internal corruption. The root-level issue. The orientation of the whole system away from its Source. This is not a thing a person does; it is a way a person is. It is the soil from which individual sins grow. Pull up one weed, and another will come. Confess one offense, and another will be committed. Because the issue is not the individual weeds. The issue is the soil. This distinction changes everything. Your sins are not the primary problem. **Your sin is**.

Behavior flows from nature. You do not become a sinner because you sin. You sin because you are operating from a corrupted nature. And no amount of effort directed at the behavior will ever fix the nature. You can, at best, get the behavior under control; you cannot get the nature restored by managing the behavior.

Why Behavior Modification Fails

If the problem were only actions, the solution would be simple: better discipline, better habits, better decisions. And humanity has tried that. Across every culture, every generation, every system of self-improvement ever devised, human beings have thrown their best effort at the problem of their own behavior. And the result is the same: temporary improvement, permanent struggle.

Why? Because behavior modification does not address source-level corruption. It is an attempt to fix outputs without touching the code that produces them. It is a compiler warning treated as if it were a syntax error — fix the compiler warning, and the program still crashes at runtime, because the real bug was somewhere else entirely.

Paul describes this exhausting internal experience vividly in Romans 7, which every honest person has, at some point, recognized as a description of his or her own life:

> *"For I know that good itself does not dwell in me, that is, in my sinful nature. For I have the desire to do what is good, but I cannot carry it out. For I do not do the good I want to do, but the evil I do not want to do—this I keep on doing."*
>
> **– Romans 7:18-19 (NIV)**

This is not the description of a lazy person. It is the description of a person who is trying. And failing. And trying again. And failing again. Because behavior modification cannot reach the source.

The Evidence of Inherited Corruption

You do not have to teach a child to lie. You do not have to teach a child to be selfish. You do not have to teach a child to resist authority. You do not have to teach a child to act out of self-interest. Every parent knows this. Every parent who has ever told a truthful child a lie has eventually found the lie circling back — unasked, unprovoked — in the child's own vocabulary. These tendencies emerge naturally.

Why? Because the system is already predisposed. This is not learned behavior. It is default programming. A child has to be taught to share. A child does not have to be taught to hoard. A child has to be trained in patience. A child does not have to be trained in demand. A child has to be shaped toward honesty. A child does not have to be shaped toward evasion.

Something is going on at a level deeper than the child's environment. Even children who grow up in loving, structured, carefully nurturing homes develop the same pattern. Even children who grow up in painful, unstable, or abusive homes show the same essential tendencies, often amplified by what has been done to them but not created by it. The environment shapes the expression. It does not create the underlying condition.

The corruption is inherited. And inherited things do not announce themselves as external invaders. They feel like us. They feel like what we have always been. Which is precisely what makes them so hard to see and so hard to address without revelation.

The Internal Conflict

Because the original design still echoes within us, there is tension. We desire good — but act against it. We seek truth — but distort it. We pursue purpose — but feel lost. We want to love — but keep acting from self-protection. We know what we should be — but cannot reach it on our own strength.

This conflict is not weakness. It is evidence of dual awareness. There is, within every human being, a memory of the original design — the echo of what we were built to be — and a reality of corrupted function — what we actually are now. These two awarenesses, running simultaneously in the same system, are why none of us is ever fully at peace with who we are. We are divided against ourselves, and the division is not random. It is structural.

Paul, in Galatians, names this explicitly:

> *"For the flesh desires what is contrary to the Spirit, and the Spirit what is contrary to the flesh. They are in conflict with each other, so that you are not to do whatever you want."*

– Galatians 5:17 (NIV)

Two systems of desire. Two orientations. Two codes. This will matter enormously when we get to the process of restoration later in the book. For now, notice only this: the tension is not a bug in your personality. It is the expected experience of a system that retains the memory of its design while running on corrupted code.

The Universality of the Condition

No one is exempt. This is one of the most confronting and most liberating truths in Scripture. It is confronting because it strips away every fantasy of moral superiority. It is liberating because it eliminates the shame of being uniquely defective.

Different people display different expressions, but the root condition is the same. Some express corruption outwardly — in visible, obvious ways, the kind that end up on the news. Some mask it internally — with reputations that are pristine and private lives that are fraught. Some refine it socially — dressing it up in politeness, respectability, even religion, so that it looks like virtue from a distance. But refinement is not restoration. A polished system is still a corrupted system.

> *"The heart is deceitful above all things and beyond cure. Who can understand it?"*
>
> **– Jeremiah 17:9 (NIV)**

This is a verse that most modern sensibilities would prefer to soften. The heart, we are told by the culture around us, is the most reliable guide we have. Follow your heart. Trust your heart. Listen to your heart. But Jeremiah — speaking from within the biblical framework — says the heart is deceitful above all things. Beyond cure. Unintelligible even to its own owner.

This is not an attack on the human heart. It is an accurate description of what has happened to the human heart. In the original code, the heart was a reliable guide, aligned to its

Source. In the corrupted code, the heart is an unreliable narrator, telling its owner stories that serve its own tangled interests. Only restoration addresses that. Management does not.

Why This Matters

If you misdiagnose the condition, you will chase the wrong cure. If you focus on sins, you will spend your life managing behavior. You will get better at not doing certain things and worse at noticing the deeper problem. If you understand sin, you will realize the need for transformation. You will stop trying to become a better version of the corrupted system. You will start looking for the Source-level solution that was always the only real solution.

This is what the prophets were calling for. It is what John the Baptist was preparing the way for. It is what Jesus came to deliver. The problem is not what you do. It is what you are operating from.

The Inescapable Conclusion

If corruption is inherited, then no one can escape it through effort. You cannot outwork your nature. You cannot outperform your condition. You cannot evolve past corrupted code. You can, if you are disciplined enough, manage it for a while. You can, if you are lucky enough, avoid some of its worst expressions. You cannot, no matter what you try, erase it from within its own operation.

Something deeper must occur. Something that does not come from within the system, but is introduced into it. Something, or Someone, that enters from outside the compromised architecture and installs what we could never install for ourselves.

That is the direction the rest of the book is moving. But first, we need to see what happens when a corrupted humanity attempts to function in real life — when the inherited corruption begins to produce its actual outputs in the actual experience of actual human beings.

Code Transmission — Breath, Procreation, and Interface

It is worth pausing, before moving on, to notice something that Scripture reveals almost quietly in its structure: the transmission of the Source Code follows a recognizable pattern across the whole biblical story. The same code can be delivered by different methods, and those methods map with surprising precision onto the history of humanity's condition. There are, in fact, four distinct transmission events that together explain how the code has moved through the human race—from its original installation, through its viral spread, into its restoration, and out into its ongoing distribution. Seeing these four in sequence does more than satisfy curiosity; it reveals an architecture that makes sense of why procreation alone cannot save the race, why rebirth is necessary, and why the church exists at all.

1. The Original Transmission — Divine Breath

The first transmission is the one we have already described at length. In Genesis, the Creator personally breathes the breath of life into the nostrils of the first human being. There are no intermediaries. The code comes directly from Source to creature. It is pure, uncorrupted, complete. Source → Human, face to face, in the garden. Every subsequent human being carries the DNA of this first download; Adam is the biological and spiritual prototype from which humanity is copied. For a moment in Eden, the only transmission pattern that existed was this one, and it worked perfectly.

> *"Then the LORD God formed a man from the dust of the ground and breathed into his nostrils the breath of life, and the man became a living being."*
>
> **– Genesis 2:7 (NIV)**

2. The Corrupted Transmission — Procreation

After the breach, however, a new transmission method takes over. Humanity is told to be fruitful and multiply, and the code continues to move—but now through procreation. One human interface connects with another human interface, and a new human being is produced. This is not, in itself, the problem; procreation is a good ordained by God. The problem is that the code being transmitted is now corrupted at the source of the copy. Adam no longer carries the uncorrupted original; he carries an infected version. And whatever a father carries is what the son receives. David states it plainly: "Surely I was sinful at birth, sinful from the time my mother conceived me" (Psalm 51:5). Humanity now reproduces not just life but condition. The interface is functioning; the file it is copying has the virus embedded.

> *"Surely I was sinful at birth, sinful from the time my mother conceived me."*
>
> **– Psalm 51:5 (NIV)**

This is why every child born on earth is loved by God and yet arrives with the same inherited problem. The transmission is happening exactly as designed; the payload is not. The Church has historically called this doctrine original sin, and whatever controversies surround the term, the underlying observation is unavoidable: we do not have to teach our children to rebel, to lie, to grasp, to fear, to fracture. These behaviors emerge on their own, because the code being transmitted from generation to generation carries a prior corruption. Procreation spreads life; it also, tragically, spreads the condition.

3. The Restoration Transmission — Divine Breath, Again

On resurrection evening, in a locked room in Jerusalem, the original transmission method returns. The risen Christ stands among His disciples and does something that echoes Genesis

2:7 with deliberate precision: "And with that he breathed on them and said, 'Receive the Holy Spirit'" (John 20:22). This is not poetry. It is re-installation. The Source, in human flesh, breathes into human beings the breath of new life. The code comes, once again, directly from Source to creature. Source → Human. Just as in the beginning. The pattern is the same; only the need has intensified, because now the breath is not merely activating dust—it is overwriting corruption.

> *"Again Jesus said, 'Peace be with you! As the Father has sent me, I am sending you.' And with that he breathed on them and said, 'Receive the Holy Spirit.'"*
>
> **– John 20:21-22 (NIV)**

4. The Ongoing Transmission — Interface to Interface

But the restored code does not stop with the disciples. A fourth transmission method now emerges—one that mirrors the structure of procreation but carries the uncorrupted payload. After Pentecost, the Spirit continues to spread through what can only be described as interface to interface: the laying on of hands, the speaking of the Word, the communal life of the gathered church. Paul is sent out by prophets and teachers in Antioch "after they had fasted and prayed, they placed their hands on them" (Acts 13:3). Ananias lays hands on Saul, and "something like scales fell from Saul's eyes" as the Spirit fills him (Acts 9:17-18).

Peter and John pray for Samaritan believers who had not yet received the Spirit, and when they lay their hands on them, the Spirit comes (Acts 8:14-17). Paul instructs Timothy to "fan into flame the gift of God, which is in you through the laying on of my hands" (2 Timothy 1:6). The pattern is unmistakable. One human interface connects with another, and the Spirit is transmitted. Unlike procreation, however, the code being passed is now the restored code, because the Source Himself is what is being carried.

> *"Then Peter and John placed their hands on them, and they received the Holy Spirit."*
>
> **– Acts 8:17 (NIV)**

> *"For this reason I remind you to fan into flame the gift of God, which is in you through the laying on of my hands."*
>
> **– 2 Timothy 1:6 (NIV)**

The Pattern Revealed

Put these four transmissions in sequence and an elegant architecture emerges. Breath gave the original code. Procreation spread the corrupted code. Breath, once again, restored it. Interface now carries the restoration forward. The method, remarkably, never changed—Source to human, human to human—only the condition of the code being transmitted. What was lost in the first interface between Adam and Eve's descendants is being recovered in the interface between Christ and His body, and between the members of that body and one another.

This is why the Church is not incidental; it is the living mechanism by which the restored code continues to spread across generations. And this is why the gospel is not private. The moment a person receives the restored code, they become, by design, a potential carrier. Transmission is built into restoration.

The reader may feel the weight of this. You have inherited a corrupted transmission; you cannot fix it by improving the copy. But you can receive a different transmission—and having received it, you can transmit it to others. The rest of the book will describe how that restoration begins and how it is carried forward. For now, it is enough to see that the God who breathed once in a garden has breathed again in a resurrection room, and the breath He gave there is moving, still, through every hand laid in prayer and every word spoken in faith.

Closing Thought

You were not just shaped by your environment. You were born into a condition. And until that condition is addressed, everything else is surface-level adjustment.

There is, in the end, something quietly merciful about this diagnosis. The condition is not your fault, in the sense that you did not generate the original corruption. You inherited it, like every other human being. The fact that you struggle is not evidence that you are uniquely broken; it is evidence that you are fully human. And the Gospel that follows in the remainder of this book is not a message of shame directed at you for being in this condition. It is a message of rescue, directed at you because you are in this condition, and you could not have escaped it on your own.

CHAPTER 05

/ THE HUMAN CONDITION

The Human Condition

Running on Altered Code

If the previous chapter explained why we are born into corruption, this chapter describes what that corruption actually looks like once it starts running its program in real life. Because the system did not stop running after the breach. It just stopped running as designed.

And that is the most disorienting feature of the post-fall human experience. You are still alive. Still thinking. Still moving. Still capable of love, of work, of art, of relationship. But beneath every one of those capacities there is a constant, low-grade malfunction — a sense that the system that is producing these outputs is not producing them cleanly. Success does not produce fulfillment. Knowledge does not produce clarity. Progress does not produce peace. Something essential has shifted in the internal operation, and the outputs are wearing the evidence.

This chapter is a diagnostic tour. Its purpose is to help you recognize, with clinical honesty, what life looks like when the source code has been altered. Not so that you can condemn yourself, and not so that you can accept the dysfunction as normal, but so that you can see clearly enough to know what restoration will have to address.

Functioning, But Not Aligned

Humanity is still active. Still thinking. Still building. Still achieving. Civilizations rise. Technologies advance. Medicine cures. Music moves. Literature illuminates. By any outward measurement, humanity is extraordinarily functional — a species capable of mapping the human genome, landing on the moon, composing symphonies, and writing the very book you are reading.

But something is consistently off. The species that mapped the genome cannot get along with its neighbors. The civilization that landed on the moon cannot keep its children safe. The culture that writes the symphony cannot bear its own silence. For every point of human flourishing, there is a corresponding point of human fracture. And the two are not distributed differently across the species. They often run through the same life.

Why? Because the system is functioning on altered code. The hardware is still capable. The operating system is still running. But the source layer — the layer that ties it all together and gives it coherent direction — is out of alignment.

The Internal Disconnect

One of the clearest signs of corrupted code is this: we often act against what we know is right.

Every honest human being is familiar with this pattern. We intend discipline and choose distraction. We desire honesty and bend truth. We pursue purpose and drift into confusion. We resolve, in the quiet of our own minds, to be patient — and within the hour, we are short-tempered with the very people we most love. We commit to stop a habit we are ashamed of — and a day later, a week later, or a year later, we are back inside of it.

This is not simply weakness. It is misalignment at the core level. The operating system mind and heart — is receiving distorted instructions from the source layer. What we actually do is often less an expression of what we have chosen than a revelation of what we are running on.

Paul captures this in the most agonizingly familiar passage in the New Testament:

> *"I do not understand what I do. For what I want to do I do not do, but what I hate I doFor in my inner being I delight in God's law; but I see another lawat work in me, waging war against the law of my mind and making me a prisoner of the law of sin at work within me. What a wretched man I am! Who will rescue me from this body that is subject to death?"*

– Romans 7:15, 22-24 (NIV)

This is not the voice of a casual sinner. This is the voice of a man who is trying. Earnestly. Desperately. And finding, in his own experience, that trying is not the same as succeeding. There are two systems at work in him. They want different things. They issue different instructions. And he is caught between them, often producing the output he did not intend and watching, with something like horror, as his own behavior contradicts his own values.

This is the human condition. Not an anomaly. The default state of every human being whose source code has not yet been addressed.

Identity Confusion

If the source code defines identity, then corrupted code produces identity instability. And identity instability is one of the most pervasive, most painful, most culturally visible features of modern life.

Watch how identity confusion expresses itself. People search for worth in achievement and then cannot rest, because the achievements are never quite enough to justify the worth. People define themselves through external validation — and then live at the mercy of a feedback loop they cannot control. People compare themselves relentlessly to others and find, no matter who they compare themselves to, that there is always someone more, always someone less, always a reason to feel inflated or diminished. People oscillate between self-aggrandizement and self-loathing, because there is no stable internal reference point to calibrate against.

When the Source is removed, identity becomes self-constructed. And self-constructed identity is always unstable. It has to be renegotiated constantly with whatever environment you find yourself in. It has to be defended against every slight. It has to be refreshed every time the culture shifts its criteria for worthiness. It has no anchor, because the anchor is precisely what was lost.

Jesus, speaking to a woman at a well in John 4, touches this exact nerve. She has had five husbands, and the man she is now with is not her husband. She has spent her life trying to construct an identity through a sequence of relationships, and by the time Jesus meets her she is emptier than when she began. He offers her not another relationship, but a source.

> *"Jesus answered, 'Everyone who drinks this water will be thirsty again, but whoever drinks the water I give them will never thirst. Indeed, the water I give them will become in them a spring of water welling up to eternal life.'"*
>
> **– John 4:13-14 (NIV)**

Everyone who drinks this water will be thirsty again. That is a description of self-constructed identity in a single sentence. The search for identity through the self always returns to thirst. The only stable identity is one that is received from the Source.

Emotional Instability as Output

The human emotional landscape, under corrupted code, is a mirror of internal misalignment. Fear replaces peace. The peace that Adam knew in the garden — the natural, unstudied ease of being in the presence of God — is not our default experience. Our default experience is wariness, vigilance, and a low-level readiness for something to go wrong. We are afraid of failure, afraid of success, afraid of being seen, afraid of being invisible. The operating system is constantly scanning for threats, because the source layer does not know, at its deepest level, that it is safe.

Anxiety replaces confidence. We live in one of the most outwardly secure civilizations in the history of the species — and anxiety disorders are at epidemic levels. This is not a contradiction. It is a confirmation. Confidence is not a function of circumstance. It is a function of alignment. A system that is aligned to its Source can be calm in a storm. A system that is not aligned cannot be calm in a penthouse.

Shame replaces security. Shame is not the same as guilt. Guilt says, I did something bad. Shame says, I am something bad. Guilt is about an action. Shame is about an identity. And shame is one of the most persistent outputs of corrupted code, because corrupted code cannot generate a stable, received identity, and in the absence of that received identity, the self becomes haunted by a feeling that it is not only failing to measure up — it is somehow, at its core, wrong.

Pride masks insecurity. This is one of the most ironic features of the corrupted system: the louder a person's self-assertion, the more likely it is that an internal fragility is being managed. Pride is almost never the behavior of a secure person. Pride is the behavior of a person who needs the world to validate something that the inner life has not been able to settle. Biblical humility is not low self-esteem; it is the easy, restful posture of someone who no longer needs to prove his worth, because his worth has been given to him by his Creator.

These are not random emotions. They are outputs of a misaligned system. They tell you something. They are not diagnoses of what is wrong with you; they are diagnostics of what is wrong with the code that is producing you.

The Illusion of Control

Humanity, confronted with internal dysfunction, tends to reach for one master strategy: control. Control through success. Control through relationships. Control through knowledge. Control through systems and structure. Control through money. Control through politics. Control through the shape of the body and the management of every detail of the environment.

The logic is understandable. If the internal world feels out of control, maybe a tightly managed external world will compensate. If I cannot quiet my own mind, maybe I can quiet my calendar. If I cannot resolve my own restlessness, maybe I can resolve my finances. Control is an attempt, at the operating-system and hardware layers, to offset what is malfunctioning at the source layer.

But control is not correction. You can manage symptoms without ever fixing the source. You can arrange the environment so skillfully that it mostly masks the internal condition. You can become a public exemplar of orderliness and a private casualty of disorder. And the gap between the arranged external and the unarranged internal becomes, over time, a kind of slow exhaustion that even the most disciplined personalities cannot outrun.

> *"There is a way that appears to be right, but in the end it leads to death."*
>
> **– Proverbs 16:25 (NIV)**

The way of control often appears to be right. It looks like maturity. It looks like responsibility. And in many of its forms, it is healthier than chaos. But as a cure for source-level corruption, control is a cul-de-sac. It manages the corruption; it cannot remove it.

The Cycle of Temporary Fixes

Because the issue is internal, humanity turns to external solutions. Achievement. Wealth. Status. Pleasure. Even religion, as we will see later. And each one of these offers real, if temporary, relief.

Achievement delivers a genuine boost. You finish the project, graduate from the school, close the deal — and for a measurable period afterward, you feel better. You feel that you have made something of yourself. You feel, briefly, like the internal contradictions might finally have been silenced. But the feeling does not last. Within weeks, sometimes within days, the old hollowness returns. You begin to think about the next achievement. The treadmill has not slowed; you have only taken one more step on it.

Wealth delivers real security — up to a point. It takes the bite out of some of life's most painful problems. But past a very low threshold, research and experience both confirm that wealth does not continue to produce proportional increases in satisfaction. A person who is wealthy and restless is just a restless person with more resources with which to distract from the restlessness.

Status delivers recognition. For a season, being known feels like being valued. But status is a game played against other people, and the other people keep changing the rules. There is no score you can post that locks in status forever. And status, once obtained, becomes something to defend rather than something to enjoy.

Pleasure is the most immediate of the substitutes, and the most fleeting. It delivers a burst of sensation and requires, with each repetition, a greater intensity to produce the same effect. This is well-documented physiologically in the mechanics of addiction, but it is equally true at the emotional and spiritual levels. Pleasure as a cure for internal emptiness produces a life of escalating appetite and decreasing return.

This is the loop of a system trying to fix itself without access to the Source: pursue, achieve, feel temporary satisfaction, return to emptiness, pursue again. The loop does not terminate. Because the loop cannot reach the source.

Why Good Isn't Good Enough

Many people assume that being good solves the problem. That if they can just become disciplined enough, decent enough, moral enough, the internal issue will quietly resolve itself. But here is the reality: good behavior does not equal restored nature.

You can be disciplined and still be corrupted. You can be kind and still be corrupted. You can be respected, admired, hardworking, high-integrity, and still be operating from corrupted code. Goodness without transformation is still self-generated output. It is still running on the same source that is producing all the other, less visible outputs. And self-generated goodness — sincere as it often is — carries its own particular forms of corruption: pride, judgment of others, quiet resentment of those who have not been as disciplined, and a secret fragility that cannot bear to be confronted with its own deeper issues.

> *"All of us have become like one who is unclean, and all our righteous acts are like filthy rags; we all shrivel up like a leaf, and like the wind our sins sweep us away."*
>
> **– Isaiah 64:6 (NIV)**

Our righteous acts are like filthy rags. This is not a claim that our good acts are worthless. It is a claim that even our best moral output, when generated by the corrupted system, is not clean enough to count as true righteousness before a holy God. The issue is not the absence of goodness. The issue is the source of the goodness.

The Fractured Self

Another effect of altered code is internal fragmentation. We live as divided selves.

There is the person you present, and the person you are. The public-facing version of you, carefully edited for consumption, and the private-facing version of you, aware of everything the public-facing version is hiding. There is the life you live, and the life you desire. The schedule you keep, and the schedule you wish you kept. The values you profess, and the values your calendar reveals. There is the image you maintain, and the reality you feel.

This creates exhaustion. Inauthenticity. A constant need to perform. Because the system is trying to hold together something that is internally divided, and holding the divided thing together takes enormous energy. The fracture is not always visible to others. But it is always felt by the one who is living it.

Jesus reserves some of His most piercing critique not for the obvious sinners of His day but for the respectable religious elite, precisely because their internal fragmentation was so well-managed that they had come to mistake the management for wholeness.

> *"Woe to you, teachers of the law and Pharisees, you hypocrites! You are like whitewashed tombs, which look beautiful on the outside but on the inside are full of the bones of the dead and everything unclean. In the same way, on the outside you appear to people as righteous but on the inside you are full of hypocrisy and wickedness."*
>
> **– Matthew 23:27-28 (NIV)**

Whitewashed tombs. A perfect image of the fractured self — clean on the visible surface, full of death on the hidden inside. This is not reserved for first-century Pharisees. It is the condition that every human being under corrupted code is, to some degree, managing.

The Echo of the Original Design

And yet, even in the corrupted state, something remains. A memory. A pull. A sense that things should be different. The desire for purpose, the longing for peace, the pursuit of truth, the need for connection — these are not random desires. They are echoes of the original source code. They are reminders that we were designed for more than this condition. The restlessness Augustine named is not the sound of a purely biological animal coping with its biology. It is the sound of a designed system remembering, at some level, what it was designed for, and knowing that it is not there.

The writer of Ecclesiastes names this beautifully:

> *"He has made everything beautiful in its time. He has also set eternity in the human heart; yet no one can fathom what God has done from beginning to end."*
>
> **– Ecclesiastes 3:11 (NIV)**

Eternity has been set in the human heart. There is a scope in us that cannot be filled by temporal things. We reach for more than the world can deliver because we were designed for more than the world is. The restlessness is not a defect. It is a signal.

Why the System Cannot Fix Itself

Here is the central issue of this chapter: a corrupted system cannot rewrite its own source code. It can adapt. It can improve. It can optimize. It cannot restore its original design.

This is not a claim about effort; it is a claim about access. Self-help has limits. Discipline has limits. Knowledge has limits. Therapy, at its most effective, has limits. All of these operate within the system — not at the source.

Imagine trying to remove a virus from a computer using only the programs that the virus itself has compromised. Whatever you run, the virus will run alongside, shaping the output, hiding its own presence, reinstalling itself through channels the compromised programs cannot see. At some level, the system needs an input from outside its own compromised framework — something the system did not write, something the system cannot corrupt, something that operates at the source layer the system cannot reach.

That is the situation of humanity. We are not lacking willpower. We are lacking a source-level solution that we cannot generate from within ourselves.

The Setup for What Comes Next

At this point, humanity reaches a critical realization. We know something is wrong. We experience the effects daily. We attempt solutions. But nothing fully resolves it. This is where something enters the story. Not to fix behavior, but to expose the problem clearly, so that the true cure can be recognized when it arrives. That something is the Law. And we turn to it in the next chapter.

Closing Thought

You are not malfunctioning randomly. You are operating exactly as a corrupted system would. That is not flattering, but it is honest, and honesty is where restoration begins.

Every symptom that you have carried — the inner contradiction, the identity instability, the emotional turbulence, the cycle of temporary fixes, the fractured public-and-private self, the persistent restlessness even in the midst of real blessing — every one of them is not evidence that you are uniquely broken. They are evidence that you are running on altered code, like every other human being, and that the code itself, not the behavior that flows from it, is what must ultimately be addressed. And until the source is addressed, the outputs will continue to reflect the code.

CHAPTER 06

/ THE LAW

The Law

A Mirror, Not the Code

By the time humanity recognizes something is wrong, a question emerges: What is the standard? What does the system look like when it is right? What are we supposed to be aiming for?

This is where the Law enters.

Why the Law Was Introduced

After the breach and the spread of inherited corruption, humanity no longer had clear internal alignment with the Source. The original code was no longer governing behavior. Cain killed Abel. Lamech boasted of his vengeance. By the time of Noah, the account says:

> *"The LORD saw how great the wickedness of the human race had become on the earth, and that every inclination of the thoughts of the human heart was only evil all the time."*
>
> – **Genesis 6:5 (NIV)**

Not some of the thoughts. Every inclination. Not some of the time. All of the time. This is what corrupted code, running unchecked for generations, produces. The internal reference point for truth and goodness has drifted so far from its source that what was once experienced as peace is now experienced as the absence of noise, and what was once experienced as goodness has to be manufactured against the grain of the default orientation.

Into that situation, God introduces something external. Not as the solution, but as revelation.

The Law.

The Law defines what is right. What is wrong. What alignment looks like. What deviation looks like. It is a perfect reflection of the original design. But it is not the design itself. And understanding that distinction is crucial if you want to avoid one of the most common spiritual mistakes of the past three thousand years.

The Giving of the Law

The Law is given most famously at Mount Sinai, after God has delivered Israel from Egypt. He calls Moses up the mountain, and for forty days Moses receives the Torah — the instruction — that will shape the life of a chosen nation.

> *"And God spoke all these words: 'I am the LORD your God, who brought you out of Egypt, out of the land of slavery. You shall have no other gods before me.'"*
>
> **– Exodus 20:1-3 (NIV)**

Notice the sequence. Before a single command is issued, the identity of the one speaking is stated, and the relationship that gives the commands their context is affirmed. I am the LORD your God, who brought you out of Egypt. The commandments that follow are not arbitrary edicts from a distant deity. They are the shape of life with the God who has already rescued them. The Law is relational before it is regulative.

The Ten Commandments are only the headline. The Torah contains hundreds of specific instructions — moral, ceremonial, civil — touching every area of communal and personal life. The purpose is not to crush Israel under a burden. The purpose is to describe what a human community aligned to God actually looks like. Every law is, at some level, a specification of what the original design would produce if human beings were running clean.

The Law as a Diagnostic Tool

Think of the Law as a mirror. It does not fix your condition. It shows you your condition. It exposes where the system is off. It reveals where corruption exists. It clarifies what the code should produce. But it has no ability to correct what it reveals.

The Law diagnoses. It does not heal.

Paul, who spent much of his life as a zealous student and defender of the Law, is one of the clearest voices on exactly what the Law is and is not meant to do:

> *"Therefore no one will be declared righteous in God's sight by the works of the law; rather, through the law we become conscious of our sin."*
>
> **– Romans 3:20 (NIV)**

Through the Law we become conscious of our sin. That is the function. Awareness. Recognition. The end of self-deception about the depth of the problem.

And elsewhere, Paul is even more direct about the mechanism:

> *"What shall we say, then? Is the law sinful? Certainly not! Nevertheless, I would not have known what sin was had it not been for the law. For I would not have known what coveting really was if the law had not said, 'You shall not covet.'"*
>
> **– Romans 7:7 (NIV)**

The Law names what would otherwise have remained unnamed. It takes the vague sense of wrongness that any honest human being carries and gives it specificity. You shall not covet — and suddenly the inner state that you had been running with all your life has a word attached to it, and the word reveals that the inner state is not a neutral feature of human experience but a specific form of misalignment.

The Law names sin. It does not remove it. Naming the disease is not curing the disease. Any doctor knows this. But you cannot cure what you have not named, and for that reason the naming is an indispensable early step.

James on the Mirror

James, in the New Testament, uses the mirror metaphor directly:

> *"Anyone who listens to the word but does not do what it says is like someone who looks at their face in a mirror and, after looking at themselves, goes away and immediately forgets what they look like. But whoever looks intently into the perfect law that gives freedom, and continues in it—not forgetting what they have heard, but doing it—they will be blessed in what they do."*

– James 1:23-25 (NIV)

A mirror cannot cleanse a dirty face. It can only show the dirt. The person looking must take the next step — find water, apply cleansing, remove the smudge. If the person merely glances, observes the dirt, and then walks away unchanged, the mirror has not failed. It has performed its function perfectly. The failure is in the viewer who treated the mirror as if it were both diagnosis and cure.

This is exactly how many people have related to the Law for centuries. They encounter the commandments, feel some measure of conviction, attempt some degree of compliance, and then proceed as if the encounter with the mirror were itself the solution. But the mirror was never meant to be the solution. It was meant to send you to the One who could do what the mirror could not.

Why the Law Could Not Fix the Problem

Here is the tension. The Law is perfect. Humanity is not. So when the Law is applied to a corrupted system, one result emerges: failure. Not because the Law is flawed — but because the system cannot meet its standard.

This is why knowing what is right does not empower you to do it. Understanding truth does not guarantee alignment. Awareness increases responsibility, but not ability. A person who has read every verse of the Bible and can quote chapter and verse is not, by that alone, running cleanly. The knowledge has been added at the operating-system level. The source layer is untouched.

Paul, in Galatians, names this limitation explicitly:

> *"Is the law, therefore, opposed to the promises of God? Absolutely not! For if a law had been given that could impart life, then righteousness would certainly have come by the law."*
>
> **– Galatians 3:21 (NIV)**

If a law had been given that could impart life... The implication is clear. No law that has ever been given can impart life. Laws do not animate. Laws do not breathe. Laws do not activate systems at the source. Laws describe. Laws reveal. Laws condemn. Laws educate. But no law — not even the Law of Sinai, the Law spoken by God Himself — is capable of reaching the source layer and restoring what the breach corrupted.

And the writer of Hebrews adds his voice:

> *"(for the law made nothing perfect), and a better hope is introduced, by which we draw near to God."*
>
> **– Hebrews 7:19 (NIV)**

The law made nothing perfect. Read that carefully. The Torah, for all its glory — for all the stunning moral vision of its prophets, the beauty of its poetry, the civilizational power of its ethics — made nothing perfect. It could not. That was not its design.

The Misplaced Hope in Performance

Humanity often responds to the Law by attempting performance-based correction. Trying harder. Doing better. Following the rules more strictly. Adding supplementary rules to the original rules, and then adding rules about how to follow the supplementary rules, until the whole system becomes an elaborate scaffolding of self-justification.

But performance cannot rewrite nature. You can conform externally while remaining corrupted internally. This is why people can follow rules, appear disciplined, maintain moral structure — and still experience the same internal conflict that the person with no such structure is experiencing, only in a more polished form. The Pharisees were the premier example of this in the Gospels. They were not bad people in the obvious sense. Many of them were serious, devoted, disciplined. But Jesus' sharpest words were reserved for them, because the very success of their external performance was obscuring — to themselves as well as to others — the unchanged condition of their source layer.

> *"For I tell you that unless your righteousness surpasses that of the Pharisees and the teachers of the law, you will certainly not enter the kingdom of heaven."*
>
> **– Matthew 5:20 (NIV)**

A staggering statement. The most disciplined law-keepers of His day were not, in Jesus' assessment, meeting the standard. Not because they were not working hard. But because the standard is not performance. The standard is restored nature.

The Woman and the Stones

There is a scene in John's Gospel that captures the entire argument of this chapter in a single courtyard confrontation. It is early morning at the temple. Jesus has been teaching, and a group of scribes and Pharisees interrupts Him by dragging a woman into the middle of the gathering. They set her before Him, and they announce the charge.

> *"Teacher, this woman was caught in the act of adultery. In the Law Moses commanded us to stone such women. Now what do you say?"*
>
> **– John 8:4-5 (NIV)**

The text is explicit about their motive. They did not come for justice. They came for a trap. John records the interior of the moment plainly: they were using this question in order to have a basis for accusing Him. The woman is an occasion. The Law is their weapon. Jesus is the target. And the whole scene is a textbook demonstration of what happens when corrupted code attempts to execute a perfect law.

Notice first that the case is already compromised before it reaches Him. The Law of Moses required the death of both the adulterer and the adulteress. The woman has been caught "in the act," which means the man was caught as well. He is conspicuously absent. The accusers have applied the Law selectively, producing an indictment that is technically partial and morally distorted. This is the characteristic signature of corrupted code running the Law: it does not reject the Law outright. It uses the Law, selectively, as a cover for agendas the Law itself would condemn.

The Mirror in Their Hands

Consider what the accusers were carrying into that courtyard. They held the mirror. They knew the specifications. They could quote the relevant commandments chapter and verse. The diagnostic tool described earlier in this chapter was in their possession, and they had lifted it up with full confidence that it authorized what they were about to do.

But the mirror was reflecting two things at once. It reflected the woman's sin, which was real. And it reflected their own corruption, which they refused to see. A mirror does not discriminate between the faces in front of it. The Law exposes every system that comes into contact with it, not only the system it is being pointed at. The accusers had forgotten this. They were treating the Law as a searchlight that could be aimed outward without illuminating the hand that was holding it.

This is why it matters that Jesus does not begin by addressing the woman. He begins by redirecting the light. And the way He does so is one of the most quietly profound gestures in all of Scripture.

Jesus Bends Down and Writes

> *"But Jesus bent down and started to write on the ground with his finger."*
>
> **– John 8:6 (NIV)**

He does not speak. He does not engage the question on their terms. He stoops. He writes in the dust with His finger.

Every detail of this action is loaded. The Law they are invoking was originally inscribed by the finger of God on tablets of stone. Now the same Finger is writing again — not on stone this time, but on the dust of the ground. The medium matters. The dust is the very substance from which humanity was formed. The LORD God formed the man from the dust of the ground, and breathed into his nostrils the breath of life, and the man became a living being. The Original Programmer is kneeling beside the substrate on which the Original Source Code was first installed. He is writing again over the material of man.

John does not tell us what Jesus wrote. Interpreters have speculated for two thousand years. Some suggest the sins of the accusers. Some suggest the relevant passages of the Law. Some suggest the names of those present. The silence of the text is deliberate. Whatever was written, the effect it produced is clear: the men who came to accuse were being confronted, silently, by the same Finger that had written the Law they were now trying to wield.

The Standard That Exposed the Room

When they persisted in questioning Him, Jesus stood up and spoke a single sentence that changed the meaning of everything that had already happened and everything that would follow.

> *"Let any one of you who is without sin be the first to throw a stone at her."*
>
> **– John 8:7 (NIV)**

Read in the frame of this book, that sentence lands at the source layer. It is not asking, Is there anyone here who has obeyed every rule? It is not asking, Is there anyone more disciplined than this woman? It is asking, in effect: Let any one of you who does not have a corrupted source code cast the first stone.

This is the standard Jesus was raising. Not behavior. Not knowledge of the Law. Not religious credentials. The condition of the inner code. The alignment of the source. The cleanness of the layer beneath every act and every thought.

By this standard, every person in that courtyard was disqualified — including the accusers who had walked in holding stones, and including the woman who had been dragged in trembling. Corrupted code cannot righteously execute perfect law. A system that is itself broken cannot be the instrument that puts another broken system to death.

The Law had named the sin. The stones were ready. But the hands holding the stones belonged to systems that were, by the very standard they were enforcing, already condemned.

The Accusers Dropped Their Stones

> *"At this, those who heard began to go away one at a time, the older ones first, until only Jesus was left, with the woman still standing there."*
>
> **– John 8:9 (NIV)**

They left one by one. The order is specified: the older ones first. The longer a corrupted code has been running, the more logs of failure it has accumulated, and the less capable it is of sustaining the illusion of righteousness when that illusion is directly challenged. The eldest had the most history to confront. They left first. The younger took slightly longer. But no one remained. Every hand that had come in ready to throw opened, and released its stone.

Notice what this scene actually demonstrates. It is not that the accusers were uniquely evil. It is that they were human. The standard Jesus named did not single them out; it exposed the universal condition. They were not worse than anyone else in Jerusalem that morning. They were simply the ones who happened to be holding the stones when the standard was spoken out loud.

This is what the Law finally does, when it is not deflected by performance or self-justification. It empties hands. It drops weapons. It strips away the pretense that there is some corner of humanity qualified to judge the rest of humanity. Corrupted code cannot condemn corrupted code. And once that truth is seen clearly, the only honest response is silence, and the slow walk away.

The Only One Left Standing

There was one person in that courtyard who could have thrown the stone. The One who had named the standard. The One whose finger had written the Law, and had just finished writing in the dust. He was, by His own specification, the only uncorrupted source present. Every other system had been dismissed by the very rule He had stated. He alone remained qualified.

> *"Jesus straightened up and asked her, 'Woman, where are they? Has no one condemned you?' 'No one, sir,' she said. 'Then neither do I condemn you,' Jesus declared. 'Go now and leave your life of sin.'"*
>
> **– John 8:10-11 (NIV)**

The One with the right to execute judgment chose not to execute it. This is not leniency. This is not a weakening of the standard. The standard has not moved. What has moved is that the only person qualified to enforce it has chosen instead to offer a different outcome. Neither do I condemn you is not what you did was acceptable. It is the stone that was yours to receive is not going to fall today. And the sentence that follows — Go now and leave your life of sin — assumes that something has shifted in her that will make a different life possible. She is not being sent back to the same corrupted firmware with a vague resolution to try harder. She is being sent away from an encounter with the Uncorrupted Source.

What This Scene Teaches the Rest of the Chapter

This moment is the argument of this chapter compressed into a single narrative. The Law was present. The Law was correctly quoted. The Law was about to be executed. And the Law, doing exactly what the Law does, exposed not only the accused but the accusers. Every system in that courtyard failed the standard the Law held up, including the systems that had arrived as enforcers.

The Law did its work. It diagnosed. It revealed. It named the disease. And when the diagnosis was complete, every hand in the room was empty, because no hand in the room belonged to a system that had the inner alignment to act on the diagnosis.

And in the middle of that silence, the One who is not corrupted was still standing. This is the direction the rest of the book is headed: not back into the performance of the Law by systems that cannot sustain it, but forward into the only solution the situation permits — an override by a Source that is not contaminated, and a rewriting of the inner code by the only hand that was never stained.

Why Even the Faithful Fell Short

Those who genuinely committed themselves to the Law — and there were many, throughout the long history of Israel — still encountered the same reality. They could not sustain alignment. Not consistently. Not completely. Not at the level of inner motive, which the Law also addressed.

Consider the tenth commandment. Nine of the ten commandments describe actions, and a disciplined person can, with effort, restrain the actions. Do not murder. Do not steal. Do not bear false witness. All of these are achievable at the behavioral layer, at least in their surface form. But the tenth commandment is different:

> *"You shall not covet your neighbor's house. You shall not covet your neighbor's wife, or his male or female servant, his ox or donkey, or anything that belongs to your neighbor."*
>
> **– Exodus 20:17 (NIV)**

This is a law about the inner life. Coveting is not an action. It is a desire. A stirring within the heart. An orientation of the will toward what is not yours to have. And here the Law begins to expose the unreachable layer — because you cannot command yourself to stop desiring. You can command yourself to stop acting on desire. You cannot command the desire itself to cease.

The Law, by including this commandment, makes it clear from the very beginning that the standard is not merely external compliance. The standard is internal alignment. And that is a standard no corrupted system can meet by its own resources.

The Law demanded perfection — external and internal, visible and invisible — and the system could not produce it. The Law showed the standard. It did not give the capacity to meet it.

The Exposure Effect

The Law does something deeper than inform. It exposes. It brings to the surface hidden motives, internal contradictions, and the gap between intention and action. It removes excuses. It eliminates ambiguity. And it makes one thing clear: the problem is not lack of knowledge. The problem is lack of alignment at the source.

This exposure effect is essential to the biblical strategy. Before people can receive a cure, they must recognize the disease. Before they can welcome a savior, they must discover that they cannot save themselves. Before they can appreciate the gift of a new source, they must exhaust the possibilities of the old source. The Law is designed to help them exhaust those possibilities — not by persecuting them, but by holding up a mirror so unflinching that no corner of the corrupted system can keep pretending everything is fine.

> *"But Scripture has locked up everything under the control of sin, so that what was promised, being given through faith in Jesus Christ, might be given to those who believe."*

– Galatians 3:22 (NIV)

Locked up everything under the control of sin. In other words, the Law has closed every avenue of self-justification, so that the only remaining option is to receive what God has always intended to give. This was never a cruelty. It was a kindness, rendered necessary by the depth of the corruption.

The Law and the Echo of the Original Code

Even in its external form, the Law reflects something familiar. It resonates. When honest people encounter the moral core of the Torah — the prohibitions on murder, theft, adultery, perjury; the positive commands to love your neighbor, to honor your parents, to care for the foreigner and the poor — something in them agrees. Not everyone will claim to have been aware of these standards before the Law named them. But once the Law names them, there is almost universal recognition that these standards are not arbitrary.

Why? Because the Law aligns with the original design embedded within humanity, dimly remembered, still dimly sensed, still producing echoes in even the most corrupted conscience. Paul notes this in Romans:

> *"(Indeed, when Gentiles, who do not have the law, do by nature things required by the law, they are a law to themselves, even though they do not have the law. They show that the requirements of the law are written on their hearts, their consciences also bearing witness, and their thoughts sometimes accusing them and at other times even defending them.)"*
>
> **– Romans 2:14-15 (NIV)**

The requirements of the law written on their hearts. The moral sense that every culture exhibits, at its best — the universal recognition that some things are actually wrong and some things are actually right — is an echo of the original code that has not been fully silenced by the corruption. The Law from Sinai makes explicit what conscience was already whispering.

But instead of restoring the original design, the Law highlights how far we have drifted from it. It is a specification document held up next to a running system, and every discrepancy between the two is visible in the light of the document.

The Breaking Point

At some point, the system reaches a realization. I know what is right. I see what is wrong. I try to correct it. But I cannot sustain it.

This is where the Law accomplishes its ultimate purpose. It removes confidence in self-repair. It strips away the fiction that a better version of yourself is just around the corner if you could only find the right discipline. It confronts you with the reality that the issue is not at the layer you have been working on, and that nothing you do at that layer is going to reach the layer that matters.

That breaking point is not a defeat. It is a door. It is the door through which the true cure can finally be received. Until that point, the cure has been interrupting an ongoing project of self-salvation; after that point, the cure can be welcomed as the very thing the system has been looking for all along.

The Transition

The Law was never meant to be the final solution. It was meant to prepare humanity for one. To move us from "I can fix this" to "I need something beyond myself."

Paul captures this role of the Law in a particularly memorable image:

> *"So the law was our guardian until Christ came that we might be justified by faith. Now that this faith has come, we are no longer under a guardian."*
>
> **– Galatians 3:24-25 (NIV)**

The Greek word translated guardian is paidagogos — a specific kind of household servant in the ancient world whose job was to supervise a child until the child reached maturity. The paidagogos was not the father. The paidagogos was not the destination. The paidagogos was the one who walked the child to school, enforced discipline, ensured safety, and brought the child ultimately into the presence of the teacher. The Law, Paul says, was this kind of guardian for humanity. Strict, but strict with a purpose. Not a final authority, but a custodian walking us toward a destination the custodian itself could not deliver.

The Promise Beyond the Law

At this point, God introduces a shift. Not more rules. Not stricter enforcement. Something entirely different. A promise. Through the prophets, a new kind of covenant begins to be described — a covenant in which the Law will no longer be primarily external, but will be written within.

> *"'This is the covenant I will make with the people of Israel after that time,' declares the LORD. 'I will put my law in their minds and write it on their hearts. I will be their God, and they will be my people.'"*
>
> **– Jeremiah 31:33 (NIV)**

This is the beginning of a new direction, and it will occupy the whole of the next chapter. For now, the point is simply this: God Himself acknowledges that the external Law was not going to be enough. Something internal must happen. The code itself must be rewritten, not just the specifications enforced. And only God can perform that rewrite. What Jeremiah is announcing here is the opening movement of the Restoration Protocol — God's commitment to do from the inside what the Law could never accomplish from the outside.

Closing Thought

The Law shows you what the code should look like. But it cannot become the code. It can expose the error; it cannot repair it. It can name the specification; it cannot execute the fix. And until the code itself is restored, the system will always fall short of the standard — no matter how long you look in the mirror, no matter how clearly you see what needs to change, no matter how earnestly you try to change it.

The mirror is doing its job. Now you are looking for the water. That is the direction the rest of the book is headed.

CHAPTER 07

/ WRITTEN WITHIN

Written Within

The Promise of Internal Code

The Law exposed the problem. It clarified the standard. It revealed the gap. It removed every illusion of self-repair. But it left one question unanswered: if the problem is internal, how will it be fixed?

God's answer was not more instruction. It was transformation. And long before the answer arrived in the person of Jesus, the prophets were already describing it, in language that becomes more astonishing the more closely you read it.

The Shift from External to Internal

Up to this point in the biblical story, everything had operated from the outside in. Commands were given. Standards were defined. Behavior was measured. Rituals of atonement covered particular failures. But the system itself remained unchanged. The Law was a teacher, a mirror, a guardian — but not a transformer. A person under the Law could have the Law memorized without having the Law become the shape of his heart.

So God, through His prophets, introduces a new promise — one that changes the direction entirely.

> *"'The days are coming,' declares the LORD, 'when I will make a new covenant with the people of Israel and with the people of Judah. It will not be like the covenant I made with their ancestors when I took them by the hand to lead them out of Egypt, because they broke my covenant, though I was a husband to them,' declares the LORD. 'This is the covenant I will make with the people of Israel after that time,' declares the LORD. 'I will put my law in their minds and write it on their hearts. I will be their God, and they will be my people. No longer will they teach their neighbor, or say to one another, "Know the LORD," because they will all know me, from the least of them to the greatest,' declares the LORD. 'For I will forgive their wickedness and will remember their sins no more.'"*
>
> **– Jeremiah 31:31-34 (NIV)**

Read that passage slowly. It is one of the most important passages in the Old Testament, and it describes a plan so radically different from the existing arrangement that even faithful Israelites must have struggled to grasp it.

A new covenant — not like the old. Not an improvement of the old, not a renegotiation of the old, but a different kind of thing. The old covenant had been broken, not because the covenant was inadequate, but because the people on the inside of it could not sustain their side of the agreement. The new covenant would be structured to avoid that failure mode by changing, not just the agreement, but the people.

I will put my law in their minds and write it on their hearts. Not on tablets of stone. On tablets of flesh. At the level of the operating system itself. The instructions would no longer sit outside the system, demanding compliance the system could not produce. The instructions would become part of the system's own internal composition.

They will all know me, from the least of them to the greatest. Not an elite mediated knowledge, accessible only through priests. A universal, direct knowledge, available to every person inside the covenant. This is a radical democratization of divine relationship made possible only by a radical internalization of divine presence.

This Is Not Symbolic Language Alone

It is easy to read Jeremiah's promise as a metaphor. As if "law written on the heart" meant only that people would be more sincere in their religion. That is not the full weight of the language. This is architectural change. Something is going to be different about the way God's people are assembled, at the level of the source layer, not just the level of their behavior.

A few chapters earlier, through the prophet Ezekiel, the picture becomes even more explicit:

> *"I will give you a new heart and put a new spirit in you; I will remove from you your heart of stone and give you a heart of flesh. And I will put my Spirit in you and move you to follow my decrees and be careful to keep my laws."*
>
> **– Ezekiel 36:26-27 (NIV)**

Read that again. Each clause is worth lingering over.

I will give you a new heart. Not a renovated heart. Not a repaired heart. A new one. The implication is that the old one cannot be fixed. It must be replaced at the level at which hearts are made.

And put a new spirit in you. At the source layer. At the deepest level. A new input installed where the compromised input used to run. Not an additional layer on top of the old. A new layer that takes the place of the old.

I will remove from you your heart of stone and give you a heart of flesh. The old heart is characterized as stone — hard, unresponsive, incapable of warming to what it should respond to. The new heart is characterized as flesh — living, responsive, able to feel and to move. This is not self-improvement language. This is transplant language. Something is being taken out. Something else is being put in its place.

And I will put my Spirit in you. The crucial clause. The Spirit of God Himself will be placed inside the human being. Not visiting occasionally. Not hovering over the situation. Indwelling. The Source, re-entering the system, but this time from the inside.

And move you to follow my decrees. Now, finally, obedience is not something the person is trying to generate against the grain of his own nature. It is something the Spirit inside him is actually producing, drawing from the person's own renewed desires, flowing from a source that no longer wants what the old source wanted.

From Observation to Installation

Under the Law, the pattern was: you read the standard, you attempt to follow it, you fall short, you try again. Under the promise, the pattern is reversed: the standard becomes part of you. Not observed. Not memorized. Installed.

The code is no longer something you reference. It becomes something you run on. This is a fundamentally different relationship to the good. In the old arrangement, the good was an external target you were aiming at and missing. In the new arrangement, the good becomes the internal pull of your own restored nature. You do not hit the target because you have gotten better at aim. You hit the target because the target is now the thing you actually want.

This is, to return to our metaphor, the difference between a rulebook stored on a server and a patched core. A rulebook stored on a server can be consulted. A patched core shapes behavior at the deepest level of execution. And what the new covenant promises is a patched core — the Original Source Code reinstalled, not merely the specifications re-read.

The Nature of Internal Code

When the Law is written within, several things begin to change at once. Obedience shifts from effort to alignment. You are no longer fighting your nature in order to do the right thing. You are doing the right thing because your nature has been changed at a level effort could never reach. Moments of obedience begin to feel less like victories won against resistance and more like the natural outflow of who you are becoming.

Desire begins to change at the source. This is the most surprising feature of the new arrangement. The things you used to want begin to lose their grip. The things you used to avoid begin, slowly, to draw you. This is not willpower at work. This is the new code, running its program, reconfiguring the default preferences of the system.

Motivation is no longer external pressure, but internal nature. You are not doing the right thing because someone is watching. You are doing it because it is now what flows out of you when no one is watching.

This is a critical shift. The goal is not to make people try harder. The goal is to make people function differently. Try-harder religion has exhausted every generation that has attempted it. Function-differently transformation is a different phenomenon entirely, and it is what the new covenant promises.

The Heart and Mind as the New Interface

God specifies two locations — the heart, which is the seat of desire, motivation, and inclination; and the mind, which is the seat of thought, reasoning, and perception. These are the two locations where corrupted code produces the most distortion, because they are the operating system layers through which source-level input is translated into behavior. So this is precisely where the rewrite begins.

What you desire begins to shift. The tug toward what was never good for you weakens; the tug toward what you were always designed for strengthens. This does not mean you never feel temptation again. It means that temptation no longer tells you the truth about what you actually most deeply want.

How you think begins to align. Thought patterns shaped by self-protection, fear, resentment, and pride start to loosen. New patterns — shaped by trust, love, mercy, and honesty — start to become available. You begin to catch yourself in thoughts you would not have questioned before, because those thoughts are now recognized by something inside you as foreign to what you are becoming.

What you pursue begins to change. The trajectory of your life — the direction your ambition leans — starts to reorient. Not because you have been lectured into it, but because the source of your ambition itself has begun to be renewed. Not because you are forcing it, but because the code governing you is changing.

Paul Picks Up the Theme

When the New Testament arrives, Paul reaches back for Jeremiah's and Ezekiel's language and applies it explicitly to what is happening through Christ:

> *"You show that you are a letter from Christ, the result of our ministry, written not with ink but with the Spirit of the living God, not on tablets of stone but on tablets of human hearts."*
>
> **– 2 Corinthians 3:3 (NIV)**

A letter written not with ink but with the Spirit. A text inscribed, not on stone, but on the tablet of the human heart. Paul is saying that the new-covenant promise of Jeremiah and

Ezekiel has arrived, and that it is being executed, in real time, in the lives of ordinary believers through the work of the Holy Spirit.

The writer of Hebrews makes the connection even more explicit, quoting Jeremiah 31 at length in the context of describing what Jesus has accomplished:

> *"This is the covenant I will establish with the people of Israel after that time, declares the Lord. I will put my laws in their minds and write them on their hearts. I will be their God, and they will be my people."*
>
> **– Hebrews 8:10 (NIV)**

The writer is not quoting Jeremiah to remind readers of an unfulfilled promise. He is quoting Jeremiah to assert that the promise has been fulfilled in the person and work of Jesus Christ. What was predicted through the prophet, what was described to a people living under the old covenant, is now the actual architecture of life inside the new covenant.

Why This Changes Everything

External systems create pressure. Internal transformation creates consistency. Under external pressure, behavior is maintained only as long as the pressure is maintained. Remove the pressure — remove the community, the accountability, the external reward and the behavior tends to drift. Under internal transformation, behavior is maintained because the person has become the kind of person who naturally behaves that way. The consistency is not fragile. It does not require constant environmental support. It is sourced from within.

When the code is within, you are no longer trying to become something. You begin to operate from what you are becoming. The difference between those two orientations is the difference between exhaustion and rest. Between striving and peace.

Between the endless self-improvement project and the actual experience of being someone new.

This eliminates the constant tension of performance. Because now the system is no longer resisting the standard. It is aligning with it.

The Beginning of True Transformation

This promise signals the beginning of something humanity had never experienced before. Not guidance from the outside, but governance from within. Not instruction addressed to a resisting heart, but the reconstitution of the heart itself.

This is the difference between modification and transformation. Between behavior and identity. Between effort and nature. Between a program that runs well as long as you keep your finger on the button and a program that has been installed as the default system.

Paul summarizes the magnitude of the shift in a sentence that rings like a trumpet:

> *"Therefore, if anyone is in Christ, the new creation has come: The old has gone, the new is here!"*
>
> **– 2 Corinthians 5:17 (NIV)**

The new creation. Not a better version of the old creation. A new one. The old has gone. The new is here. This is the language of architectural replacement, not of incremental improvement.

Heart of Stone and Heart of Flesh — The Receiving System

There is one more image in Ezekiel's prophecy that must not be rushed past, because it names the deepest layer of the human problem. The issue is not merely that the code is corrupted; the issue is also that the system trying to receive any code has been rendered unresponsive. God does not only promise new code; He promises a new heart. "I will give you a new heart and put a new spirit in you; I will remove from you your heart of stone and give you a heart of flesh" (Ezekiel 36:26). The language is deliberate. Stone does not bend, does not grow, does not receive an imprint without being shattered. Flesh is alive, pliable, responsive. The distinction between the two describes not two kinds of religious sentiment but two kinds of receiving system.

> *"I will give you a new heart and put a new spirit in you; I will remove from you your heart of stone and give you a heart of flesh."*
>
> **– Ezekiel 36:26 (NIV)**

The Heart of Stone — A Static System

Scripture describes the natural human condition, post-fall, as a heart of stone. In system terms, it is rigid. Unresponsive. Resistant to change. The analogy of a hard drive with corrupted sectors fits precisely: data cannot be written properly, instructions fail to store, and the same errors repeat no matter how many times the user tries to re-enter them. Everyone who has tried to change a deep pattern in their own life by willpower alone has encountered the heart of stone. You can read the right book, hear the right sermon, sign the right commitment card, and still find, three weeks later, that nothing has been written at the operating-system level. The surface flickered; the stone did not move.

Zechariah describes the same tragedy in historical terms: "They made their hearts as hard as flint and would not listen to the law or to the words that the LORD Almighty had sent by his Spirit through the earlier prophets" (Zechariah 7:12). Flint is stone of a particular quality—capable of striking a spark, but incapable of being written upon. The prophets stood in front of their generations, speaking true words, and those words struck the flint and ricocheted. This is the condition of every human system before the rewrite begins. Information cannot become transformation when the receiving surface cannot be inscribed.

> *"They made their hearts as hard as flint and would not listen to the law or to the words that the LORD Almighty had sent by his Spirit through the earlier prophets."*

– Zechariah 7:12 (NIV)

The Heart of Flesh — A Writable System

God's promise, then, is not a patch but a hardware replacement. He does not offer to update the stone; He offers to remove it and install something that can actually receive what He wants to write. A heart of flesh is alive. It is responsive. It is writable in the most literal sense: the Spirit can now inscribe new instructions that will actually be stored, actually be run, and actually produce output that matches the input. The user who has spent years typing truth into a stone heart and watching it evaporate will, upon receiving a heart of flesh, discover that the same truths now stick. The sermon that bounced off for decades is suddenly heard. The verse that was familiar is suddenly alive. The counsel that once felt impossible is suddenly possible. Not because the code is newer; because the receiving system is new.

Now the Code Can Be Written

This is what makes the whole promise of the new covenant operative. God does not simply send a better transmission; He also installs a better receiver. Both sides of the communication must work for the code to reach the system. And this is where the mechanical language must be married to the relational one: a heart is not a machine part.

A heart is the center of a person. When Scripture says God gives a heart of flesh, it is saying that the core of the person—

the place where affections form, where decisions are made, where love responds to love—has been restored to the kind of openness it was designed to have from the beginning. You were made to be responsive to your Maker. Stone is not your original state; it is the damage the virus did. The heart of flesh is a return to what you were meant to be before the hardening set in.

The pastoral implication here is urgent. If you are reading this and you feel that truths about God bounce off you, that sermons move others but leave you cold, that you cannot seem to make spiritual disciplines take root, the problem is not that you are too far gone. The problem may be that you are still trying to write on a stone heart. The promise of Ezekiel is precisely for you. God's solution is not more effort applied to flint; it is a new heart given to the one who asks. Ask Him for it. The Spirit who raised Jesus from the dead—the Spirit who is the agent of Ezekiel 36—can still soften what has been hardened and still make writable what has been sealed shut. The problem was never just the code. It was also the system trying to receive it. And once both are addressed, the rewrite can finally begin.

The Bridge to Fulfillment

The promise of Jeremiah and Ezekiel did not stand alone. It pointed forward. Because for the Law to be written within, something had to happen first. The corrupted nature had to be addressed. A new nature had to be introduced. The system had to receive new source input. And that would require an intervention from outside the compromised architecture someone who was not himself corrupted, someone who could open a channel the old system could not open for itself.

This is where the whole arc of the Old Testament points: toward the One through whom the promise would be fulfilled. The One whose arrival the prophets anticipated. The One in whose coming the new covenant would be inaugurated. The

One whose Spirit would be the very presence inside the restored system.

That One is Jesus. And the remainder of this book will trace what His coming accomplishes: the incompatibility between corrupted humanity and holy God that He alone can bridge (Chapter 8), the rebirth He offers (Chapter 9), the Holy Spirit He sends as the agent of ongoing restoration (Chapter 10), and the process of continuous override by which the new code progressively becomes the default operation of the restored system (Chapter 11 and beyond).

Closing Thought

The solution was never more rules. It was always a new internal reality. A system where the code is no longer something you chase, but something you carry. A life where the voice of God is not a distant instruction you struggle to obey, but an indwelling Spirit producing, from within, the very obedience you used to fail to achieve.

This was promised by the prophets. It was anticipated for centuries. It was realized in Christ. And it is offered, today, to any system ready to stop chasing the external code and ready to receive the internal one.

CHAPTER 08

/ INCOMPATIBILITY

Incompatibility

Why Corruption Cannot Stand Before Holiness

By this point in the book, a pattern has become clear. The system was designed perfectly. The breach introduced corruption. That corruption was inherited. The Law exposed it, but could not fix it. A promise was given to rewrite the code internally. Now we arrive at a critical truth: transformation is not optional. It is required.

It is required not because God is capricious. Not because He is offended by our particular failings and demands that we clean up our act before He will associate with us. It is required for a reason that goes deeper than preference. It is required by the nature of the One we are dealing with.

Holiness as a Perfect System

To understand why transformation is required, we must understand the nature of God. And the key word is one that modern ears often mistranslate.

Holy.

In Hebrew, qadosh. In Greek, hagios. The word is often treated as if it were a religious synonym for moral—as if saying that someone is holy were only a slightly dressed-up way of saying that they are very good. That is not what the word means. Holy, at its root, means set apart. Different. Other. Belonging to a category of its own.

When God is described as holy, the claim is not that He is at the high end of a scale that also includes us. The claim is that He is off the scale. Not higher in degree. Different in kind. Not the best example of something we also are; but the one and only example of something that is unique to Him.

The prophet Isaiah, receiving a vision of God's throne, does not describe a slightly more impressive version of an earthly court. He describes something so thoroughly other

that the creatures around the throne sing of holiness as the defining attribute of the One seated on it:

> *"And they were calling to one another: 'Holy, holy, holy is the LORD Almighty; the whole earth is full of his glory.'"*
>
> – **Isaiah 6:3 (NIV)**

Three times. In Hebrew literature, tripling a word is the highest emphasis possible. God is not just holy. He is not just very holy. He is holy to the third degree — holy in a way that exceeds any scale of holy we can measure. The seraphim cannot catalog it. They can only repeat it.

The Reality of Exposure

In our framework, holiness is a perfect system environment. Nothing within it is misaligned. Nothing within it is distorted. Nothing within it operates outside of truth. Every element in the environment functions cleanly and in full alignment with every other element. There is no conflict within it. There is no deviation within it. There is no decay within it.

And a corrupted system cannot function in a perfect environment. Not because it is rejected arbitrarily, but because it is incompatible by nature.

Isaiah, in the same vision, immediately discovers this. He does not stand in the throne room and congratulate himself on his religious achievements. His instinctive reaction is unlike anything he has ever said before:

> *"'Woe to me!' I cried. 'I am ruined! For I am a man of unclean lips, and I live among a people of unclean lips, and my eyes have seen the King, the LORD Almighty.'"*
>
> **– Isaiah 6:5 (NIV)**

I am ruined. That is not a polite confession of minor imperfection. That is the cry of a man whose corrupted code has just come into direct contact with a holy environment, and who has instantly understood that he cannot exist in this environment as he currently is. He has not been told about his corruption. He has simply, finally, been exposed to something clean enough that the contrast cannot be ignored.

When corrupted code is brought into the presence of perfect code, two things happen simultaneously. Every flaw is exposed. Every distortion is revealed. There is no hiding. No masking. No performance strong enough to cover the gap. This is why, throughout Scripture, encounters with God's presence are overwhelming. Not because God is hostile, but because His perfection exposes everything that is not aligned.

Notice the pattern in Scripture. Moses, face to face with God, must veil his face afterward because his skin is glowing with residual glory. Ezekiel, encountering the likeness of the glory of God, falls face down. Daniel, receiving a vision, loses his strength entirely. Peter, in the boat after the miraculous catch of fish, falls at Jesus' knees and says, "Go away from me, Lord; I am a sinful man!" John, on the island of Patmos, encountering the risen Christ, falls at His feet as if dead. This is not religious theater. This is the natural reaction of corrupted systems to unshielded exposure to source-level holiness.

Why the System Crashes

In human terms, we might say: a corrupted system entering a perfect environment results in system failure.

The language of Scripture often describes this as death — not merely physical, but the inability to sustain presence in holiness. When God warns Moses in Exodus, the warning is direct:

> *"But, he said, 'you cannot see my face, for no one may see me and live.'"*
>
> **– Exodus 33:20 (NIV)**

This is not because God wants to harm anyone. It is because what is corrupted cannot endure what is perfect. The system in its current state is not structurally able to exist in that environment. Exposure is not cruelty. It is physics.

Consider, as an imperfect analogy, the experience of walking out of a dimly lit room into direct sunlight. The sun is not malicious. It is simply bright. But your eyes, accustomed to lower light, cannot immediately process the intensity. You squint, you turn away, you shield your face. The sun has done nothing to you; its presence has merely exposed the difference between your current state and the environment you have entered.

Now extend that analogy by an infinite order of magnitude, and move it from the level of optical adjustment to the level of moral and spiritual reality. Corrupted code cannot stand in the environment of perfect code. Not because the perfect code has a grudge. Because the corrupted code has no structural integrity in that light.

Not Rejection — Reality

It is important to understand: this is not about God pushing humanity away. It is about what humanity has become.

This is one of the most frequent misunderstandings in conversations about God and judgment. People imagine that the problem is somehow on God's side — that He is picky, exclusive, unwilling to tolerate. But Scripture presents the problem on the other side. God's presence is exactly what humanity was designed for. It is not God's nature that has changed; it is humanity's nature. If the system were restored, there would be no barrier. God has not moved. We have.

The prophet Habakkuk puts it this way:

> *"Your eyes are too pure to look on evil; you cannot tolerate wrongdoing."*
>
> **– Habakkuk 1:13 (NIV)**

Not "Your eyes are too scornful." Not "Your eyes are too judgmental." Too pure. Too clean. Too aligned to the truth to be able to treat corruption as anything other than what it is. That is not a flaw in God's character. It is a feature of His holiness. And it is precisely what humans, once healed and restored, will one day love about Him — the absolute reliability of a God in whom there is no shadow, no compromise, no corruption of any kind.

The Old Covenant Example

Under the old system, access to God's presence was limited. The tabernacle, and later the temple, had an inner room called the Holy of Holies. This most sacred space could not be entered freely. Only the high priest could enter, and only once a year, on the Day of Atonement, and only with elaborate preparation sacrifice, ritual purification, incense, a rope tied around the ankle so that he could be pulled out if he were struck dead inside.

This was not arbitrary ritual. It was a living object lesson. God's presence, in its undiluted form, could not be approached casually by a corrupted people. The barriers and the layers of the temple were a visible theology: the further in you went, the more strictly the conditions of access applied, because the closer you drew to holy presence, the more the condition of your own code mattered.

> *"But only the high priest entered the inner room, and that only once a year, and never without blood, which he offered for himself and for the sins the people had committed in ignorance. The Holy Spirit was showing by this that the way into the Most Holy Place had not yet been disclosed as long as the first tabernacle was still functioning."*
>
> **– Hebrews 9:7-8 (NIV)**

The architecture of the temple was itself preaching. It was telling the people, generation after generation, that access to God was real, but not automatic. That corruption and holiness cannot coexist without something happening at the source layer. That the whole arrangement of limited access was itself an invitation to anticipate something more — a day when the barriers would come down, not by lowering the holiness, but by restoring the worshipers.

Until then, holiness could not be approached with corrupted code.

The Weight of the Standard

This creates a tension humanity cannot resolve on its own: the desire to connect with God runs into the inability to meet the standard required for that connection. No amount of effort bridges that gap. Because the issue is not distance. It is nature.

You cannot walk far enough, climb high enough, or purify yourself ritually enough to become structurally compatible with perfect holiness. Walking is a function of the operating system. Climbing is a function of the hardware. Ritual purification, at best, addresses the operating system layer and leaves the source layer untouched. The gap between corrupted and holy is not a distance to be covered. It is a kind of difference — a kind of incompatibility — that cannot be closed from our side.

> *"Surely the arm of the LORD is not too short to save, nor his ear too dull to hear. But your iniquities have separated you from your God; your sins have hidden his face from you, so that he will not hear."*
>
> – Isaiah 59:1-2 (NIV)

Your iniquities have separated you. The separation is not a punishment God imposes; it is a reality iniquity produces. And it cannot be undone by the iniquitous party deciding to behave better going forward. The structural incompatibility remains until the source of the iniquity has been healed.

Why Transformation Is Required

At this point, the conclusion becomes unavoidable. The problem is internal. The standard is absolute. The gap is unbridgeable through effort.

Therefore, the system must be changed at its core. Not adjusted. Not improved. Changed.

This is the reason a Savior was ever necessary in the first place. If the issue were behavior, a teacher would suffice. If the issue were ignorance, a book would suffice. If the issue were environment, a new country would suffice. But the issue is nature, and only a new nature will do — a new nature that restores compatibility between humanity and the holiness of God.

Jesus names this requirement in unmistakable terms in Hebrews:

> *"Make every effort to live in peace with everyone and to be holy; without holiness no one will see the Lord."*
>
> – Hebrews 12:14 (NIV)

Without holiness, no one will see the Lord. That is as direct as the New Testament ever is. It is not cruel. It is not restrictive. It is architectural. The vision of God is not an experience a corrupted system is capable of. It is an experience that only a restored system — a system made holy — can have.

The Necessity of a New Nature

For humanity to exist in alignment with God, corruption must be removed. Original design must be restored. A new governing code must be introduced. This is why rebirth is not a suggestion. It is a requirement.

Jesus says this to a leading religious figure of His day — a man who has kept the Law as faithfully as any Pharisee could, a man whose outward life is probably impressive by every human standard:

> *"Jesus replied, 'Very truly I tell you, no one can see the kingdom of God unless they are born again.' ... Jesus answered, 'Very truly I tell you, no one can enter the kingdom of God unless they are born of water and the Spirit. Flesh gives birth to flesh, but the Spirit gives birth to spirit. You should not be surprised at my saying, "You must be born again."'"*
>
> **– John 3:3, 5-7 (NIV)**

Notice what Jesus does not say to Nicodemus. He does not say, "You are a pretty good man; a little polishing and you will be fine." He says the same thing He would say to any other person in Jerusalem that day, or any person in your city today: you must be born again. The condition of incompatibility runs so deep that only a new birth — a new beginning, a new source, a new nature — can address it.

We will unpack the meaning of that new birth in the next chapter. For now, it is sufficient to notice that Jesus treats rebirth as a universal necessity. Not reserved for the egregious sinners. Not optional for the morally accomplished. A universal requirement for anyone who intends to see the Kingdom of God.

Closing Thought

You cannot bring corrupted code into a perfect system and expect it to function. You cannot stand before holiness while running on a compromised internal framework. Something must change, and that change must begin at the deepest level of who you are.

This is not an inconvenient footnote to the Gospel. This is the whole reason the Gospel is the shape it is. If the requirement were merely that we behave better, Christianity would be one more religion of self-improvement among many. It is not. It is the announcement of something only God can do the announcement of a rebirth, a new nature, a restored compatibility with the holiness we were originally designed to live in. And that announcement, once rightly understood, is not bad news. It is the best news ever proclaimed to a species that cannot solve its own most foundational problem.

CHAPTER 09
/ REBIRTH

Rebirth

The Reinstallation of the Original Code

Everything up to this point has led here. The system was designed perfectly. The breach introduced corruption. That corruption became inherited. The Law exposed the problem. Holiness revealed the incompatibility. Now the question is no longer what is wrong. The question is: what fixes it?

And before we can describe how the system is rebuilt, one prior truth must be established, because without it nothing else in this book finally lands. Every human system born after the breach carries corrupted code. No matter how refined, how disciplined, how externally successful, how religiously observant or morally earnest, every descendant of Adam inherits the same infection at the source layer. This raises a question so simple that most people never ask it, and so decisive that once it is asked, nothing else can be answered without it. If every system is corrupted, where does a clean system come from? It cannot come from within the system. A corrupted source cannot generate uncorrupted code. However refined the output, the output will still carry the signature of the source that produced it. For an uncorrupted system to exist in this world at all, something, or someone, must enter the compromised architecture from outside it.

The Perfect Code — The Entry of the Uncorrupted System

This is where Jesus Christ enters the story, and this is the order in which the Bible asks us to receive Him. Not, first of all, as a teacher. Not, first of all, as a moral example. Not, first of all, as the founder of a religious movement. He is all of those things in the end, but He is more fundamentally something else: He is the only human life that has ever run the Original Source Code without corruption. He is, in the most architectural sense possible, an uncorrupted system entering a corrupted world. Everything else the New Testament says about Him depends on this being true. Remove this claim, and Jesus becomes one more well-meaning teacher in a long line of well-meaning teachers, all of whom were running the same virus as the people they tried to help. Keep this claim, and Jesus becomes the single data point that changes what the rest of humanity can know about itself. The design is not broken. The copy is broken. And there is now, in history, one copy that is not.

Not Born Through the Corrupted Line

Every other human being, from Adam forward, receives code through procreation, and with that procreation receives the inherited corruption that Adam passed on. Scripture is unembarrassed about this; it is simply how the transmission has worked since the breach. But when the Gospels describe the arrival of Jesus, they describe something unprecedented. Luke records the angel Gabriel's answer to Mary's question about how this could possibly be:

> *"The angel answered, 'The Holy Spirit will come on you, and the power of the Most High will overshadow you. So the holy one to be born will be called the Son of God.'"*
>
> **– Luke 1:35 (NIV)**

The Holy Spirit will come on you. Matthew frames the same event from Joseph's side, noting that "what is conceived in her is from the Holy Spirit" (Matthew 1:20). This is not a minor theological flourish. This is the architectural claim that Jesus does not enter the species through the ordinary transmission alone. The Source Himself is involved at the point of origin. If He were produced only through the corrupted line, He would carry the same corrupted code that the rest of us do, however remarkable His teaching. But He is not. He enters the system without the infection. This is why the writer of Hebrews can make a claim that would be absurd applied to anyone else: "For we do not have a high priest who is unable to empathize with our weaknesses, but we have one who has been tempted in every way, just as we are—yet he did not sin" (Hebrews 4:15). Tempted like us, but without corruption. A real human being, in a real human body, running on code that had never been compromised.

> *"For we do not have a high priest who is unable to empathize with our weaknesses, but we have one who has been tempted in every way, just as we are—yet he did not sin."*
>
> **– Hebrews 4:15 (NIV)**

Perfect Alignment — No Internal Conflict

Because the code is uncorrupted, the life looks different. Throughout the Gospels, Jesus describes Himself in a way that, if it came from any other mouth, would sound either psychotic or absurdly self-aggrandizing: He claims to do only what He sees the Father doing. Not most things. Only those things. "Very truly I tell you, the Son can do nothing by himself; he can do only what he sees his Father doing, because whatever the Father does the Son also does" (John 5:19). A few verses later: "By myself I can do nothing; I judge only as I hear" (John 5:30). And later still: "For I have come down from heaven not to do my will but to do the will of him who sent me" (John 6:38). This is not merely obedience.

Any number of devout people have attempted obedience. This is something rarer. This is perfect synchronization with the Source. No distortion between input and output. No internal contradiction. No competing inner voice pulling in another direction. No corrupted processing layered between the signal from God and the response from the man. Where the rest of humanity is double-minded, Jesus is single-aligned. Where we struggle to make our inner life match our outer profession, He simply flows. The code inside Him is running; and because it is running without the virus, what flows out of Him is what the Source intended to flow out of human life all along.

The Second Adam — A New Starting Point

Scripture presents Jesus not only as a Savior who rescues individuals, but as a replacement starting point for the human race. Adam stands at the head of a corrupted humanity; Jesus stands at the head of a new humanity. Paul makes this architectural:

> *"For just as through the disobedience of the one man the many were made sinners, so also through the obedience of the one man the many will be made righteous."*
>
> **– Romans 5:19 (NIV)**

One man's disobedience introduced corruption into the species. One man's obedience introduces righteousness into a new species. This is not a metaphor stretched beyond its reach; it is the way Paul actually reasons about what has happened in Jesus. What Adam broke at the source level, Jesus restores at the source level. The first Adam began a line of corrupted code; the second Adam begins a line of restored code. Every person born of Adam inherits what Adam passed on. Every person born again in Christ begins receiving what Christ passes on. Two humanities, running two codes, traceable back to two heads. That is the cosmic geometry the New Testament is working with, and Jesus sits at the head of the new geometry.

A Life That Proves the System Works

Because His code is perfect, Jesus does not merely speak truth; He demonstrates what a human system looks like when the code is not corrupted. In Him we see love without selfishness, because love is not being routed through self-protection. We see power without corruption, because power is not being redirected toward self-aggrandizement. We see authority without control, because authority is not being used to dominate those beneath it. We see identity without confusion, because His sense of who He is does not wobble in front of the crowd's praise or the crowd's hatred. We see peace without internal war, because nothing inside Him is fighting against itself. This is not Jesus trying to behave correctly. This is Jesus functioning correctly. The difference is the whole point. Corrupted humans, at our best, manage the symptoms of the virus; Jesus simply does not have the virus to manage. Looking at Him, humanity is not being crushed by an impossible example. Humanity is being shown what it was designed to be, in the only form it could be shown: lived out, in a real human body, on real dusty roads, in front of witnesses who could not make Him up.

The Interface Responds to Perfect Code

Because His source is uncorrupted, even the interface—the body, the material world around Him, the fabric of what we call nature—responds differently when He speaks. He speaks, and bodies are restored. He touches, and sickness leaves. He commands, and wind and sea fall silent. This is not magic, and it is not a special-effects sequence meant to dazzle. It is alignment. When the code is perfect, the interface follows. We will return to this more carefully later, because the Bible never turns this into a formula and never promises that alignment erases every illness in every believer's life in this present age. But it is honest to say, here, that when perfect code meets hardware, hardware responds in ways corrupted code has never been able to produce. In Jesus, for a few short years, the interface of this world glimpses what it was made to do when it is met by a source that is not broken. The lame walk. The blind see. Storms obey. This is not Jesus overpowering nature. This is nature finally hearing its native language.

Not Just an Example — An Entry Point

This is why reducing Jesus to a teacher to follow, or a model to admire, misses what the New Testament actually claims about Him. The solution to corrupted code is not imitation. A corrupted system imitating an uncorrupted system is still a corrupted system; it can mimic the outputs for a while, but it cannot change its source. The solution is not imitation. The solution is installation. Jesus does not come primarily to give humanity a better pattern to copy. He comes to make Himself the only access point to restored code and to offer to run that code through anyone who will receive Him. "Remain in me, as I also remain in you. No branch can bear fruit by itself; it must remain in the vine. Neither can you bear fruit unless you remain in me" (John 15:4). He does not say, try harder to produce my kind of fruit. He says, stay connected to me and my kind of fruit will appear. Paul says it in even more architectural language: "Christ in you, the hope of glory" (Colossians 1:27). Not Christ beside you, not Christ above you as a remote standard, but Christ in you. The Perfect Code, not merely displayed, but installed.

> *"Remain in me, as I also remain in you. No branch can bear fruit by itself; it must remain in the vine. Neither can you bear fruit unless you remain in me. I am the vine; you are the branches. If you remain in me and I in you, you will bear much fruit; apart from me you can do nothing."*
>
> **– John 15:4-5 (NIV)**

> *"To them God has chosen to make known among the Gentiles the glorious riches of this mystery, which is Christ in you, the hope of glory."*
>
> **– Colossians 1:27 (NIV)**

The Restoration Begins the Same Way It Started

In the beginning, God bent down over the dust of the first man and breathed, and the dust became a living being. After the resurrection, Jesus, in a locked room with disciples who are grieving and afraid, does something that the Gospel of John wants His readers to see very clearly. He breathes. "And with that he breathed on them and said, 'Receive the Holy Spirit'" (John 20:22). This is not a symbolic gesture. This is not stage direction. This is intentional. The restoration of humanity begins the exact same way the original started through breath. At Genesis 2:7, the Source exhaled life into dust. At John 20:22, the Source exhales life into disciples. The action is deliberately rhymed. The book of Genesis has a new chapter, and it is being written with the same verb. What began with breath is being restarted with breath.

> *"Again Jesus said, 'Peace be with you! As the Father has sent me, I am sending you.' And with that he breathed on them and said, 'Receive the Holy Spirit.'"*
>
> **– John 20:21-22 (NIV)**

From Breath to Network

And once the restored code is received, it begins to travel. The disciples who received the breath begin to transmit what they have received. Acts is the long record of this transmission: hands are laid on new believers, and the Spirit comes; the gospel is preached, and people are born again; interfaces become carriers of the same restored code, which spreads from Jerusalem to Judea to Samaria to the ends of the earth. The transmission system that once carried corrupted code from generation to generation is not abolished; it is reclaimed. Only now the code being transmitted is no longer corrupted. It is restored. The same network, now carrying a different signal.

Why This Changes Everything

Before Jesus, humanity had corrupted systems and a Law that diagnosed the problem but could not fix it. The Law could tell you what health looked like; it could not put it in you. It could show you the distance between the virus and the ideal, but it could not close that distance. Now, for the first time since Eden, a perfect system has appeared. A new pattern is visible. A new starting point is introduced. And because that new starting point is a person who lives and breathes and can be received, the offer on the table is no longer, "try harder with the broken code you already have." The offer is, "receive a new source, who will begin living His life from inside your life, and whose code will, over time, rewrite the defaults you have been running on since your first breath."

The problem was never that humanity stopped running. We have been running for a very long time. The problem is that humanity has been running on corrupted code. And in Jesus, for the first time since the beginning, the Original Source Code is running again in a human being—fully, perfectly, without error. That is the anchor of this chapter and the anchor of everything the rest of the book is going to say. What the next sections describe—rebirth, the indwelling Spirit, a new core identity, the beginning of real transformation—is simply how this perfect code, now alive in the world, becomes alive in you.

And the answer the Bible gives is so radical that even a learned teacher of Israel, hearing it for the first time, had to stop Jesus mid-sentence and ask what He could possibly mean.

Not Improvement — Replacement

The solution is not self-improvement. Not discipline. Not education. Not external conformity. None of those reach the source layer. The answer is far more radical. The system must be **born again**.

In Gospel of John chapter three, this is stated plainly, in the middle of a nighttime conversation between Jesus and Nicodemus, a member of the Jewish ruling council. Nicodemus comes in the dark, offering a cautious compliment: "Rabbi, we know that you are a teacher who has come from God. For no one could perform the signs you are doing if God were not with him." It is the kind of opening that might lead to a friendly theological exchange. Jesus does not give Nicodemus that exchange. He cuts straight to the architecture:

> *"Jesus replied, 'Very truly I tell you, no one can see the kingdom of God unless they are born again.'"*
>
> **– John 3:3 (NIV)**

Not upgraded. Not repaired. Reborn.

Nicodemus hears the word "born" and, understandably, stumbles on the obvious absurdity of taking it literally. "How can someone be born when they are old? Surely they cannot enter a second time into their mother's womb to be born!" And Jesus, without softening, doubles down:

> *"Jesus answered, 'Very truly I tell you, no one can enter the kingdom of God unless they are born of water and the Spirit. Flesh gives birth to flesh, but the Spirit gives birth to spirit. You should not be surprised at my saying, "You must be born again."'"*
>
> **– John 3:5-7 (NIV)**

Flesh gives birth to flesh. That which is born of biological procreation inherits the flesh — the corrupted nature. It is possible to be physically healthy, mentally sharp, socially admirable, and spiritually still dead, because the only birth that has happened is the kind of birth that passes on corrupted code. A second birth is required. A birth of a different order entirely. A birth from water and the Spirit.

Why Birth, Not Repair

Birth implies origin. Birth means a new beginning. A new nature. A new source. You do not fix what was corrupted. You introduce something new. This is not the only time the Bible reaches for the language of birth to describe what God does in a person through the Gospel. Peter uses it as well:

> *"For you have been born again, not of perishable seed, but of imperishable, through the living and enduring word of God."*

– 1 Peter 1:23 (NIV)

Born again. Not reformed. Not recycled. Born. From a different kind of seed than the one that produced your first birth. Your first birth gave you a perishable life, with all the inherited corruption that came with it. This second birth delivers an imperishable life, grounded in a different source, running on code that is not subject to decay.

James says something similar from a different angle:

> *"He chose to give us birth through the word of truth, that we might be a kind of firstfruits of all he created."*

– James 1:18 (NIV)

He chose to give us birth. The initiative is not ours. This is an important feature of the new birth: you do not perform it on yourself. You did not perform your first birth, either. The first birth was handed to you, without your consent, by parents you did not choose. The second birth is given to you by a Father you did not choose, but who has chosen you. In both cases, being born is something that happens to you, not something you execute.

Paul puts it even more strikingly:

> *"he saved us, not because of righteous things we had done, but because of his mercy. He saved us through the washing of rebirth and renewal by the Holy Spirit."*
>
> **– Titus 3:5 (NIV)**

The washing of rebirth. A complete, cleansing inaugural moment. Not an improvement project. Not an earned promotion. A washing.

Natural Birth vs. Spiritual Birth

It helps to compare the two births side by side.

Natural birth receives inherited corrupted code. It begins life within the broken system. It operates from compromised nature. It is the entry point into the Adamic condition — a condition no one chose, but into which everyone is conceived. Natural birth is a gift, and it is good; but it does not, by itself, deliver what we truly need. It delivers a person who will live, for a time, within a system that is not functioning as designed.

Spiritual birth is initiated by God. It introduces new source input. It establishes a new governing nature. It is the entry point into the new creation — a category of life that did not exist at your first birth. It is not a religious veneer laid over the top of the natural life; it is a different kind of life altogether. Scripture has a specific vocabulary for this new kind of life: zoe in Greek, often translated life, the word used when Jesus says, "I am the way, the truth, and the life," or when John writes, "In him was life." This zoe is not mere biological animation. It is the life of God made available to the human being.

This is not symbolic. It is actual transformation at the core level.

The Greatest Born of Women

There is a sentence Jesus speaks about John the Baptist that, read through the lens of this chapter, lands with extraordinary precision. It appears in Matthew's Gospel, in the middle of a conversation about the nature of the kingdom and John's place within its arrival. Jesus has just been defending John to the crowds, calling him a prophet and more than a prophet. Then He says this:

> *"Truly I tell you, among those born of women there has not risen anyone greater than John the Baptist; yet whoever is least in the kingdom of heaven is greater than he."*
>
> **–– Matthew 11:11 (NIV)**

This is not a statement about personal virtue. Jesus is not saying that people in the kingdom are more disciplined than John, more devoted than John, or more spiritually experienced. John was consecrated before his birth. He lived in radical simplicity. He preached with fearless conviction in the wilderness and prepared the way of the Lord. By any measure of character and commitment, he represents something extraordinary. He is, in fact, the ceiling — the highest output the old system, operating through natural birth and the corrupted replication mechanism, has ever been able to produce.

And yet the least person in the kingdom surpasses him. Not because they are a better person than John. But because they are running on a different system entirely. They have been born again. The Original Source Code has been reinstalled. The Restoration Protocol that John announced — but stood on the near side of — has been applied to them. The corrupted replication mechanism delivered them into the world, as it delivered John. But something happened after that: a second birth. A different transmission. A source that natural birth alone could never carry.

This is the very distinction this section has been drawing. Natural birth, however consecrated and however Spirit-touched from the outside, still enters the world through the inherited, corrupted condition. John was filled with the Holy Spirit from his mother's womb — the Spirit was upon him, but not yet fully within him in the new covenant sense. Kingdom citizens have the Spirit installed inside them. The firmware has been replaced. The source layer has been reconnected. What was true of Jesus — that the Spirit governed Him from within is now, by grace, true of every person who has been born again.

If you have been born of the Spirit, hold this truth carefully. You are not greater than John because you are better. You are greater because of what has been installed in you — the same breath that activated the first human at the beginning, now made available to you through the new covenant. John announced that One was coming whose sandals he was not worthy to untie. By the grace of the new birth, you are now indwelt by that very One.

The Moment of Activation

After the resurrection, something remarkable happens in the Gospel of John. Jesus appears to His disciples in a locked room. They are grieving. They are afraid. They are still processing the impossible reality that their crucified rabbi is alive again. And in the middle of this meeting, He does something ancient:

> *"Again Jesus said, 'Peace be with you! As the Father has sent me, I am sending you.' And with that he breathed on them and said, 'Receive the Holy Spirit.'"*
>
> **– John 20:21-22 (NIV)**

He breathed on them.

This is not an incidental detail. This is an echo the gospel writer wants you to hear clearly. At the beginning of creation, God bent down and breathed into the dust of man, and man became a living being. Now, at the beginning of the new creation, the risen Christ breathes on His disciples and says, "Receive the Holy Spirit." The verbs are the same in the underlying language. The posture is the same. The action is the same.

This is not coincidence. This is recreation. The breath that activated the original humanity is now being exhaled into the new humanity. The Source Code is being reinstalled, not this time by shaping dust, but by breathing into disciples already shaped by their first birth and now being prepared for their second. Just as humanity was first activated by breath in Genesis, now a new humanity is activated the same way.

Every detail of the scene underlines the parallel. Locked doors open. Fear turns to peace. Death-bound people become commissioned. And the signal of the whole transformation is a breath.

The Holy Spirit as Source Input

The Holy Spirit is not an external force. He is the return of the Source. Not beside you, but within you. This is what changes everything, because now the system is no longer operating alone. The original code is reintroduced. A new nature begins to govern.

Paul, describing the result of this in the Christian, writes:

> *"You, however, are not in the realm of the flesh but are in the realm of the Spirit, if indeed the Spirit of God lives in you. And if anyone does not have the Spirit of Christ, they do not belong to Christ. But if Christ is in you, then even though your body is subject to death because of sin, the Spirit gives life because of righteousness. And if the Spirit of him who raised Jesus from the dead is living in you, he who raised Christ from the dead will also give life to your mortal bodies because of his Spirit who lives in you."*
>
> **– Romans 8:9-11 (NIV)**

The Spirit of God lives in you. Not visits. Lives. The same Spirit who raised Jesus from the dead is now the indwelling source of life in the reborn person. This is a claim so large that it is almost reckless — and yet Paul makes it with absolute confidence. It is the central architectural fact of a Christian. Not that they have chosen to adopt a new set of beliefs. Not that they have joined a new community. Not that they have improved their morals. But that the Spirit of the living God now indwells them.

A New Core Identity

At the moment of rebirth, identity is no longer defined by the corrupted system. A new internal reality is established. The foundation shifts from self to Source. You are no longer just a product of inherited nature. You become a participant in restored design.

Paul uses a striking phrase to capture this. He calls the Christian "in Christ" — over and over, throughout his letters, this phrase appears. To be in Christ is to have a new defining context for your life. Your identity is no longer exhausted by your history, your personality, your achievements, or your failures. Your identity is now set inside a new reality: you are a person in whom Christ lives, and who lives in Christ.

> *"I have been crucified with Christ and I no longer live, but Christ lives in me. The life I now live in the body, I live by faith in the Son of God, who loved me and gave himself for me."*
>
> **– Galatians 2:20 (NIV)**

I no longer live, but Christ lives in me. This is the most explicit architecture statement Paul ever makes about the born-again life. It is not a mystical exaggeration. It is a sober statement of what has happened at the source layer. The old self — the self that was defined by inherited corruption — has been reckoned dead. A new self, with Christ indwelling, has replaced it. The life now being lived in the body is a life lived by faith in a Christ who is inside the one doing the believing.

What Rebirth Is — and What It Is Not

Rebirth is a spiritual activation. A new source connection. A shift in internal identity. It is real, and it happens at a specific moment, even if that moment is not always remembered with photographic clarity.

Rebirth is not instant perfection. It is not immediate behavioral completion. It is not the removal of all struggle. The new code is introduced, and it is the code that will, over time, come to govern the system. But the old patterns do not evaporate at the moment of installation. The old habits, learned reactions, ingrained preferences, still press for attention. The memory of how you used to think, what you used to want, how you used to react, is still present. The body you live in still carries the accumulated weight of years of operation under the old code.

Rebirth is a beginning. Transformation is the ongoing process. We will turn to that process in the chapters that follow. For now, hold onto the distinction. Rebirth is the inaugural event. It is real, complete, and final — you will not need to be born a third time. But the implications of your rebirth unfold progressively across the rest of your life, as the new code gradually rewrites the defaults of the system it has entered.

The Beginning, Not the End

At the moment of rebirth, the new nature is installed. The old system begins to be challenged. Transformation begins from within. This leads, almost immediately, to tension. Old patterns vs. new identity. Old habits vs. new desires. Old code vs. new code. This tension is not failure. It is evidence that the rewrite has begun. A life in which nothing is being contested is a life in which the new code has not yet made itself felt. A life in which old patterns are being confronted in which old habits suddenly feel unworthy of you, in which old ways of thinking start to sound foreign in your own ear — is a life in which the new source is doing exactly what new sources are supposed to do.

Why This Changes Everything

Before rebirth, you try to become something you are not. You are operating from corrupted code, and the corrupted code cannot produce what you are trying to produce. Every effort at self-improvement runs into the same ceiling.

After rebirth, you begin to live from what you are becoming. You are operating on new code, and the new code, over time, will progressively deliver outputs that the old code could not produce. Effort does not disappear; but the nature of effort changes. You are no longer trying to generate what is not in you. You are cooperating with what is now in you.

This is the difference between striving and transformation. Striving is the attempt to produce a different life from the same source. Transformation is the experience of a different source producing a different life.

Paul's Summary

When Paul summarizes the whole of the Christian identity, he does not reach for the language of achievement. He reaches for the language of creation.

> *"Therefore, if anyone is in Christ, the new creation has come: The old has gone, the new is here!"*
>
> **– 2 Corinthians 5:17 (NIV)**

The old has gone. The new is here. It is the language of Genesis applied to the individual person. What God did at the beginning of the universe — calling forth what was not — is what He has now done at the beginning of your new life. Not renovated you. Created something new in you. Brought forth, out of the dust of an old and corrupted humanity, a new kind of humanity, breathing with His own breath, animated by His own Spirit, bearing His image in a way that the old humanity could no longer bear.

The Design Made Visible

It is worth pausing on one more angle of this, because it is the hinge on which the reader's confidence rests. Without a perfect example walking among us, humanity would only have two reference points: the corrupted version of itself, and the standard of the Law. Looking at ourselves, we would see only the virus. Looking at the Law, we would see only the distance between the virus and the ideal, and we would have no living demonstration that the ideal was ever possible. Jesus removes that doubt. He is the Word made flesh—the design made visible, walking among us, eating and drinking and sleeping and weeping in a real first-century body, yet running without corruption.

> *"The Word became flesh and made his dwelling among us. We have seen his glory, the glory of the one and only Son, who came from the Father, full of grace and truth."*

– John 1:14 (NIV)

The writer of Hebrews puts it in language a software engineer would recognize: "The Son is the radiance of God's glory and the exact representation of his being, sustaining all things by his powerful word" (Hebrews 1:3). The phrase translated "exact representation" is charaktēr in the original Greek—the impression left by a stamp or a seal pressed into wax. Jesus is the exact impression of the Source in human form.

Looking at Him, we are not guessing at what God is like, and we are not guessing at what uncorrupted humanity would look like if it still existed. We are seeing both, in the only form we could receive them: a man who lived, and breathed, and touched lepers, and cried real tears, and was, from start to finish, the exact impression of the code humanity was originally designed to run. This is the anchor. The life you were made for is not a theory. It has been lived. And the One who lived it is now offering, by His Spirit, to begin walking it in you.

> *"The Son is the radiance of God's glory and the exact representation of his being, sustaining all things by his powerful word."*

– Hebrews 1:3 (NIV)

Closing Thought

You cannot fix corrupted code by trying harder. You need a new beginning. You need a new source. You need to be born again. And the staggering claim of the Gospel is that the One who breathed the first breath into the dust of man has, in Christ, breathed the second breath into any who will receive it. The Source is not distant. He is offering to become the source of your life again — not to restart the old code, but to install a new one, alive with His own life, carrying you, step by step, back toward the original design He has never stopped intending for you.

CHAPTER 10

/ THE HOLY SPIRIT

The Holy Spirit

The Restoration Protocol

Rebirth introduces the new code. But introduction is not completion. A system can receive new code and still carry remnants of the old. So the question becomes: how does the new code take over? How does the installed Spirit begin actually to produce the life He is there to produce?

The answer is the ongoing work of the Holy Spirit Himself. Rebirth gave Him entry.

Now He begins to govern.

More Than Presence — Active Restoration

The Holy Spirit is not passive. He is not symbolic. He is not occasional. He is active – continually working within the system to restore alignment with the Original Source.

In John's Gospel, Jesus prepares His disciples for the coming of the Spirit in detailed, relational language. He does not describe the Spirit as a force or an impersonal power. He describes the Spirit as a person who will come and stay.

> *"And I will ask the Father, and he will give you another advocate to help you and be with you forever—the Spirit of truth. The world cannot accept him, because it neither sees him nor knows him. But you know him, for he lives with you and will be in you."*
>
> **– John 14:16-17 (NIV)**

Another advocate. The Greek word is parakletos – one called alongside. An advocate, a counselor, a helper. The prefix another is important: another of the same kind as Jesus

Himself. The Spirit Jesus promises is not a lesser substitute. He is the continuing, indwelling presence of the same God who walked among them in the flesh, now reaching inside each one of them in a form the world cannot access but the reborn can.

Rebirth installs the new nature. The Spirit ensures it begins to govern.

From External Control to Internal Guidance

Before restoration, behavior is driven by impulse, habit, environment, and external pressure. The person goes wherever the strongest current pushes — whether that is the pull of appetite, the momentum of routine, the expectations of those around them, or the fear of consequences. There is no internal compass reliably calibrated to truth. The loudest voice wins, and the loudest voice is almost never the wisest one.

After the Spirit enters, guidance becomes internal. Conviction replaces mere awareness. Direction becomes clear from within. This is not control from the outside. It is leadership from the inside.

> *"For those who are led by the Spirit of God are the children of God."*
>
> **– Romans 8:14 (NIV)**

Led by the Spirit. Not coerced. Not steamrolled. Led — the way a shepherd leads, or a father leads, or a guide leads. The Spirit does not override your will and drag you where you do not want to go. He works in you to make you want what is good, and then He leads you in following through on what you have, by His own work inside you, come actually to want.

This is what Jesus promises in another passage:

> *"But when he, the Spirit of truth, comes, he will guide you into all the truth. He will not speak on his own; he will speak only what he hears, and he will tell you what is yet to come."*
>
> **– John 16:13 (NIV)**

He will guide you into all the truth. This is not a one-time illumination. It is an ongoing guidance. Day by day, moment by moment, the indwelling Spirit leads the believer into deeper understanding of reality — of God, of self, of Scripture, of the path forward. The believer does not become omniscient. The believer becomes correctly oriented.

Conviction — The First Sign of Rewrite

One of the earliest signs of the Spirit's work in a person is conviction. Not condemnation. Not shame. Conviction is clarity. The difference between conviction and condemnation is worth spelling out carefully, because the two are often confused.

Condemnation says, "You are bad. You are hopeless. You are unlovable. You have always been this way and always will be." Condemnation points at the person and declares them defective. Condemnation leaves no way forward. It crushes.

Conviction says, "This is not who you are now. This thought, this action, this pattern does not belong to the new code. You are being invited to leave it behind, and the help to leave it behind is already inside you." Conviction points at specific misalignments, names them with accuracy, and offers a way through them. Conviction wounds in order to heal.

Jesus describes the Spirit's ministry of conviction this way:

> *"When he comes, he will prove the world to be in the wrong about sin and righteousness and judgment."*
>
> **– John 16:8 (NIV)**

Prove the world to be in the wrong. The Greek verb elencho carries the sense of bringing something into the light, exposing what was hidden, giving something a clear and accurate assessment. This is what conviction does. You begin to see what is misaligned. You recognize patterns that contradict your new nature. You feel tension where there was once comfort. This is the system becoming aware of its own misalignment so that the alignment can actually be adjusted.

Paul contrasts godly conviction and worldly shame precisely:

> *"Godly sorrow brings repentance that leads to salvation and leaves no regret, but worldly sorrow brings death."*
>
> **– 2 Corinthians 7:10 (NIV)**

Two very different feelings, both of which can involve tears and inner weight. Godly sorrow is the Spirit's conviction doing its work. Worldly sorrow is shame without direction the recognition of failure without the path out. The Spirit never leaves a person in worldly sorrow. He never lands the diagnosis without also offering the remedy. The conviction is always followed by invitation: turn, change, and receive the help that is already inside you.

The Conflict Between Codes

Once the new code is introduced, two systems exist simultaneously in the believer. The old corrupted nature — Paul calls it the flesh — and the new restored nature — often simply called the Spirit, or the new self. This creates conflict.

> *"For the flesh desires what is contrary to the Spirit, and the Spirit what is contrary to the flesh. They are in conflict with each other, so that you are not to do whatever you want."*
>
> **– Galatians 5:17 (NIV)**

Old desires vs. new desires. Old habits vs. new direction. Old identity vs. new identity. This is not failure. It is evidence that the system is being rewritten. In the unregenerate person, the flesh rules unchallenged; there is no conflict because there is no competing voice. In the regenerate person, a new voice has arrived, and the conflict that was absent before is now present, precisely because a restoration is underway.

This is surprising to many new believers. They expect that after rebirth, life will become smoother, not more contested. In some ways it does; but in other ways, it becomes more contested than it was before, because now there are two codes competing for the defaults of the system. That competition is uncomfortable. But it is the very sign that the new code has entered and is pressing the system toward alignment.

Paul immediately follows the conflict verse with a reassurance:

> *"But if you are led by the Spirit, you are not under the law."*

– Galatians 5:18 (NIV)

You are not under the law. You are no longer in the old system, where external rules demand what internal nature cannot deliver. You are in a new system, where the internal Spirit produces what the external law pointed at. The conflict is real, but the trajectory is settled: the Spirit is moving you, step by step, toward the life He Himself is authoring inside you.

The Role of Surrender

The Spirit does not force control. He works through alignment and cooperation. This introduces a critical principle: transformation accelerates where surrender exists.

Surrender is not weakness. In the New Testament, the posture of the believer toward the Spirit is never passive in the sense of limp. It is active yielding. It is the deliberate act of releasing control of the system and allowing the Source to govern.

> *"Do not offer any part of yourself to sin as an instrument of wickedness, but rather offer yourselves to God as those who have been brought from death to life; and offer every part of yourself to him as an instrument of righteousness."*
>
> **– Romans 6:13 (NIV)**

Offer every part of yourself. Every part. Not the parts you find it easy to hand over, but every part — including the parts you have privately decided you will keep under your own management. These are the very parts where surrender is most needed and where transformation most dramatically accelerates when surrender actually happens.

Paul elsewhere puts it this way:

> *"Therefore, I urge you, brothers and sisters, in view of God's mercy, to offer your bodies as a living sacrifice, holy and pleasing to God—this is your true and proper worship."*
>
> **– Romans 12:1 (NIV)**

A living sacrifice. Not something killed once on an altar, but something given continuously, every day. This is the posture in which the Spirit's work is most fully experienced. You trust. You yield. You allow the process of restoration. You cooperate with the rewrite rather than resisting it.

Rewriting the Operating System

The Spirit works primarily through the mind and heart. Thought patterns begin to shift. Desires begin to realign. Perception becomes clearer. What once felt normal begins to feel off. What once felt distant begins to feel natural. This is the operating system being updated.

Paul is explicit about this in Romans:

> *"Do not conform to the pattern of this world, but be transformed by the renewing of your mind. Then you will be able to test and approve what God's will is—his good, pleasing and perfect will."*
>
> **– Romans 12:2 (NIV)**

Do not conform — do not keep running the default program of the world around you. Be transformed — the Greek word is metamorphoo, the word from which we get metamorphosis. A caterpillar-to-butterfly level of change. A change of kind, not just degree. How? By the renewing of your mind. The mind is one of the main locations where the Spirit's rewrite becomes visible. Old assumptions are replaced by new ones. Old patterns of interpretation yield to new ones. Old reactions lose their grip as new ones take root.

As this renewal unfolds, something surprising happens: you discover you can now test and approve what God's will is. What once seemed arbitrary begins to seem reasonable. What once seemed restrictive begins to seem protective. What once seemed distant begins to seem intimate. The renewed mind does not merely obey God's will; it begins to perceive God's will as good, pleasing, and perfect. The Spirit is reorienting not just your behavior, but your very categories of evaluation.

Gradual Override — Not Instant Replacement

The restoration process is not immediate completion. It is a continuous override.

Old code is challenged. New code is reinforced. Patterns are replaced over time. This explains why change can feel slow. Why growth requires consistency. Why progress happens in stages. The Spirit is not in a hurry to finish you by next Tuesday. He is in a process of forming you into someone who can bear His likeness for eternity, and that kind of formation is not rushed.

> *"being confident of this, that he who began a good work in you will carry it on to completion until the day of Christ Jesus."*

– Philippians 1:6 (NIV)

He who began a good work in you will carry it on to completion. The sentence has a structure. He began it. He will carry it on. He will finish it. The responsibility for completion does not fall on you. Your responsibility is cooperation with the One who is doing the work. Your job is not to finish the rewrite. Your job is to yield to the rewriter.

The Difference Between Behavior Change and Transformation

Behavior change is external, temporary, and effort-driven. Transformation is internal, progressive, and source-driven.

The Spirit does not aim merely to modify behavior. He aims to change the system that produces behavior. Many Christians, misunderstanding this, fall into a kind of religious behaviorism — a life focused on controlling actions while leaving the source layer largely unaddressed. The result is often a life that looks disciplined on the outside and feels exhausting on the inside, because the work is being done at the wrong layer.

Paul's instruction in Galatians is clarifying:

> *"So I say, walk by the Spirit, and you will not gratify the desires of the flesh."*

– Galatians 5:16 (NIV)

Notice the sequence. He does not say, "Stop gratifying the desires of the flesh, and you will be walking by the Spirit." He says the opposite. Walk by the Spirit, and you will not gratify the desires of the flesh. The inner walk produces the outer restraint. The external discipline is the fruit, not the root. This is a completely different approach to change than the world normally offers. The world says, "Fix your behavior and you will become a better person." The Spirit says, "Let Me make you a new person, and your behavior will begin to follow."

The Fruit of the Spirit — Behavioral Output of Restored Code

If the restoration of the Source Code is actually happening in a person, it will not remain invisible. Real code produces real output. A system that has been rewritten at the core will, over time, produce behavior that reflects what is now running inside. Scripture calls this behavioral output the fruit of the Spirit, and Paul lists it in one of the most quoted passages of the New Testament:

> *"But the fruit of the Spirit is love, joy, peace, forbearance, kindness, goodness, faithfulness, gentleness and self-control. Against such things there is no law."*
>
> **– Galatians 5:22-23 (NIV)**

Output, Not Effort

The word Paul chooses is decisive. He does not say, "But the achievements of the Spirit are love, joy, peace..." He says fruit. Fruit is not manufactured; fruit is produced. You do not force fruit onto a tree; you cultivate the conditions—the soil, the water, the root, the sunlight—and fruit, in time, appears. A mango tree does not strain to produce mangoes; when the mango tree is healthy, mangoes are simply what happens. In the same way, the fruit of the Spirit is the natural output of a life in which the Spirit is actively doing the work of restoration. You do not generate these qualities by willpower; you cooperate with the Spirit who generates them, and over time they emerge.

This matters, because Christian life lived under the wrong metaphor becomes exhausting. If a believer thinks that love, joy, peace, patience, and the rest are tasks to be performed, she will perform them with the same fractured resources that could not perform them before and she will burn out. If she understands them as fruit, she will shift her attention away from forcing the output and toward tending the conditions in which the Spirit can work. She will spend time in the Word. She will pray. She will gather with the body of Christ. She will confess sin. She will submit her will. She will, in short, tend the root. And the fruit, to her quiet surprise, will begin to appear.

Evidence of Correct Function

These nine traits are not, in the deepest sense, religious traits. They are system outputs. They are the visible signature of a human being running on the uncorrupted code. Where they are present, the Source is active. Where they are absent, something is wrong at the core, and no amount of surface polish will produce them. Jesus said it starkly: "By their fruit you will recognize them" (Matthew 7:20). Not by their vocabulary. Not by their religious credentials. Not by their claimed experiences. By what the life, over time, actually produces.

> *"Thus, by their fruit you will recognize them."*
>
> **– Matthew 7:20 (NIV)**

Every one of the nine deserves a brief description, because the labels are so familiar that their meaning can slip away from the reader. Love, in Paul's vocabulary, is not sentiment but agapē—the committed, self-giving orientation toward others that characterizes God Himself. Joy is not emotional high; it is the stable gladness that does not depend on circumstance because it is sourced in the unchanging Source. Peace is not the absence of conflict around you; it is the absence of fragmentation within you—internal alignment with God producing interior wholeness. Forbearance (patience, makrothumia) is the capacity to wait under pressure without erupting, because the one waiting is no longer ruled by the tyranny of the immediate.

Kindness is the disposition to do good to others without calculation of return. Goodness is the integrated moral substance of a soul whose interior matches its exterior. Faithfulness is the consistency that can be trusted over time; it is the trait of a system whose output does not drift from its stated intent. Gentleness is strength held in restraint—power under the governance of love. And self-control is the restored capacity to govern one's appetites rather than be governed by them. These are not nine unrelated virtues; they are the unified signature of a life whose core has been reconnected to the Source.

From Forced Behavior to Natural Expression

Before restoration, every one of these qualities must be forced. Love is strained, peace is pretended, patience is manufactured for as long as the muscle can hold, self-control is maintained by gritted teeth until exhaustion breaks it. The unregenerate system can produce brief imitations of the fruit—anyone can be kind for an afternoon—but cannot sustain them, because the source is not in the system.

After restoration, the dynamic changes. Love begins to flow where once it had to be dragged. Peace begins to settle where once it had to be faked. Self-control begins to rise as a natural capacity, not as a battle for every inch of ground. Not perfectly, not instantly, but progressively and consistently. The believer is surprised to find that she responded gently in a moment that, two years ago, would have produced an explosion. The Spirit has been working.

This is what the book has meant, throughout, when it has spoken of transformation rather than modification. Modification would leave the old reluctance in place and layer new behaviors on top of it. Transformation changes the reluctance itself. The old hatred weakens, not because it has been suppressed, but because a new love has been planted in its place and is slowly out-competing it. The old anxiety loosens its grip, not because it has been muscled aside, but because a new peace has been poured into the same interior that the anxiety used to fill alone. The fruit is not performed for God; it is produced by God, through the believer, into the world.

The Indicator of Transformation

This gives the believer a reliable, non-religious way to test whether the rewrite is actually happening. The question is not, "Do I have the right theology?" but, "What is consistently being produced through me?" The question is not, "Do I attend the right services?" but, "Over the arc of a year, is there more love in my life than there was a year ago? More peace? More patience? More self-control?"

The fruit test is slow; it cannot be run on an afternoon, and it requires the honesty of people close to us who actually see what we produce. But it is the test Jesus Himself named, and it is the test that keeps Christian discipleship from being reduced to vocabulary or performance. What is consistently produced reveals what is internally operating. If the fruit is growing, the Spirit is at work. If the fruit is absent across years, something is wrong at a level that no more effort will fix—and the invitation is to return to the root, to the Source, and to ask for the rewrite to deepen.

It is worth saying, pastorally, that the fruit does not grow evenly in every believer. Some believers receive joy quickly but struggle for years with patience. Others are made gentle from the first day but grow in self-control slowly. The Spirit knows each system and works in each one with wisdom. The point is not perfection at any given moment; it is the direction of the trajectory. Over time, all nine begin to emerge, because they are nine facets of one Spirit, and the Spirit who is at work does not leave His work half-finished. "He who began a good work in you will carry it on to completion until the day of Christ Jesus" (Philippians 1:6). The fruit that is only beginning now will ripen. The Spirit who has started is faithful to finish.

> *"Being confident of this, that he who began a good work in you will carry it on to completion until the day of Christ Jesus."*
>
> **– Philippians 1:6 (NIV)**

Living From the New Nature

As the Spirit's work continues, decisions begin to align naturally. Desires shift toward what is right. Resistance decreases over time. You are no longer forcing alignment. You are functioning from it.

This does not mean temptation disappears. It does not mean the old patterns never show up again. It means the old patterns are no longer dictating. The new code is increasingly the default, and the old code is increasingly the exception. What once was the exception — moments of genuine alignment with God — becomes the baseline. What once was the baseline — the old reactions, the old orientations — becomes the exception.

This is not self-congratulation. It is description. A tree that has been watered for ten years looks different from a tree that has just been planted. A life that has been submitted to the Spirit for a decade looks different from a life that was born again yesterday. The difference is not the believer's achievement. The difference is the Spirit's work. But the work is real, and it shows.

Why This Process Cannot Be Replaced

No system outside of the Spirit can produce this level of change. Not discipline. Not knowledge. Not structure. Not therapy. Not any of the real and sometimes useful modalities available to the human being.

This is not to disparage those modalities. Each of them can be genuinely helpful at the levels at which they operate. Discipline shapes behavior. Knowledge informs the mind. Structure provides external scaffolding for habits. Therapy heals wounds and unpacks patterns. All of these are good and can be useful. But none of them operates at the source level. None of them can install what was lost in the breach. None of them can breathe the breath of God into a system whose original breath has been silenced.

Only the Source can restore the system. And the Source does so through the person of the Holy Spirit, indwelling those who have been born again in Christ.

Closing Thought

Rebirth starts the process. The Spirit sustains it. And over time, what was once corrupted begins to reflect the Original Design again.

This is the Restoration Protocol. Not a technique you execute on yourself. Not a discipline you master. But a Person who has entered the most intimate place in you, who loves you too much to leave you as He found you, and who is quietly, patiently, relentlessly rewriting every misaligned line of your source code until what He is doing in you is finally complete in the day when everything that has ever gone wrong in this world is made right.

CHAPTER 11

/ THE PROCESS

The Process

Continuous Override

Rebirth is the beginning. The Spirit is the agent. But transformation unfolds over time. Not in a single moment of completion, but in a process of continuous override.

Many people come into the Christian life expecting instant completion. They hear about the new birth, the new creation, the new nature, and they assume — not unreasonably — that these things will produce an instantly different life. And in some ways they do. There is often an initial experience of joy, relief, clarity, even astonishment, in the early days of a newly reborn life. But as the weeks and months unfold, a different reality also sets in. Old patterns show up again. Old desires stir again. Old reactions break through in moments of pressure. And the new believer wonders whether the rebirth was real after all.

It was real. The instant completion was not the model. The process is.

Why the Rewrite Is Not Instant

When new code is introduced, it does not immediately replace every existing function in the system. The system still carries old patterns, old responses, and old habits. These were built over time, and they must be replaced over time.

The new code is perfect. The system applying it is still being restored. This is not a defect of the code. It is a feature of the restoration. Instant, forced overrides would bypass the person, and God is not willing to bypass you. He is unwilling to produce a transformation that has not, at the deepest level, been yours.

Paul captures this tension clearly:

> *"Therefore, my dear friends, as you have always obeyed—not only in my presence, but now much more in my absence—continue to work out your salvation with fear and trembling, for it is God who works in you to will and to act in order to fulfill his good purpose."*

– Philippians 2:12-13 (NIV)

Two agencies, working together. You work out your salvation. God works in you. The Christian life is not passive, and it is not self-powered. It is cooperation — a real human effort, continuously enabled by a real divine indwelling. The Spirit does not dispense with your choices. He shapes the desires from which your choices spring.

Two Systems, One Life

After rebirth, there is an ongoing tension. The old nature is still present. The new nature is now active. Both attempt to influence thoughts, desires, and decisions. This is why transformation feels like a battle. Not because something is wrong, but because something is changing.

Paul calls these two systems by many names across his letters — the flesh and the Spirit, the old self and the new self, the law of sin and the law of the Spirit of life. They are not equal forces. The new has come with a decisive advantage; the decisive victory has already been won in Christ. But the old system does not disappear overnight, and its voice continues, weaker over time but persistent, inside the life of the believer.

> *"Do not lie to each other, since you have taken off your old self with its practices and have put on the new self, which is being renewed in knowledge in the image of its Creator."*

– Colossians 3:9-10 (NIV)

Two verbs to notice. You have taken off your old self — past tense. That is done. The identity is no longer "old self." You have put on the new self — past tense. That is also done. The identity is "new self." But the new self is being renewed — present continuous. The identity is settled; the formation of the identity is ongoing. The past tense verbs describe what has happened at the source layer. The present continuous describes what is happening at the operating system layer and the behavioral layer as the source rewrite propagates through the rest of the system.

The Nature of Override

Override is not deletion. It is replacement through repetition and alignment. The old response arises. The new code challenges it. A choice is made. The system reinforces what it follows.

Over time, what is reinforced becomes default. This is how neural pathways form in the brain, and it is a reasonable analogy for how character forms in the soul. The first time you respond to an old trigger with a new response, it takes effort. It feels awkward. You can almost feel the old pattern being resisted. The twentieth time, it is easier. The hundredth time, the new response is arriving before you have to think about it. The thousandth time, the new response is the default — and the old response, when it occasionally still tries, feels like the awkward one.

This is the way the Spirit works. He does not usually erase memory of the old patterns. He writes new patterns on top of them, more and more deeply, until the new pattern has become the road of least resistance and the old pattern has become an overgrown, unused path through the woods.

Repetition Creates Rewiring

The system changes through consistent alignment. New thoughts replace old patterns. New decisions replace old habits. New desires begin to take root. What once required effort begins to feel natural. This is the shift from forced behavior to internal alignment. You stop waking up every morning feeling as if you have to earn the day by sheer willpower. You start waking up already oriented, already wanting what aligns with the Source, already finding the old options less appealing than they used to be.

Paul points to this dynamic in Ephesians:

> *"You were taught, with regard to your former way of life, to put off your old self, which is being corrupted by its deceitful desires; to be made new in the attitude of your minds; and to put on the new self, created to be like God in true righteousness and holiness."*
>
> **– Ephesians 4:22-24 (NIV)**

Put off. Be made new. Put on. These are not one-time events. They are ongoing actions, repeated in ten thousand small moments over the course of a lifetime. Each one is small. Each one feels almost negligible at the time. But accumulated across years, they are the means by which the new self, already present at rebirth, becomes the lived experience of the believer.

The Role of Awareness

Transformation requires awareness. You must recognize what belongs to the old system and what aligns with the new nature. This awareness grows through reflection, sensitivity to conviction, and exposure to truth.

Without awareness, the system defaults to old programming. Many Christians live for years without experiencing much transformation, not because the Spirit is inactive in them, but because they are not cooperating with awareness. They do not slow down enough to notice what they are thinking. They do not sit still long enough to hear what the Spirit is saying. They do not read Scripture consistently enough to have truth available when their own hearts begin to drift. The Spirit is still at work; but the cooperation that accelerates the Spirit's work is missing.

> *"But solid food is for the mature, who by constant use have trained themselves to distinguish good from evil."*

– Hebrews 5:14 (NIV)

Trained themselves. By constant use. Spiritual discernment grows like a muscle. Every time you pause, notice, and choose alignment rather than drift, the muscle grows stronger. Every time you fail to pause, notice, and choose, the muscle is left untrained. The Spirit is willing and able to train you. But training, by its nature, is a process that unfolds over time and requires your engaged participation.

The Role of Time

There is no shortcut to deep transformation. Time allows patterns to be broken, new pathways to form, and stability to develop. This is why patience is essential. Immediate change is visible. Lasting change is built.

Consider the language of Scripture. The Christian life is described as running a race. Growing a harvest. Completing a building. Maturing in wisdom. None of these images suggests instant completion. All of them suggest sustained investment over time.

> *"And we all, who with unveiled faces contemplate the Lord's glory, are being transformed into his image with ever-increasing glory, which comes from the Lord, who is the Spirit."*

– 2 Corinthians 3:18 (NIV)

Being transformed. Present continuous. With ever-increasing glory. Not transformed once and finished. Being transformed, and increasingly so, for the whole of a believer's life. This is not evidence that something is wrong with the process. This is the shape of the process, and it is a good shape. If you were finished transforming, there would be nowhere further to grow. You are still transforming because the horizon of God's glory is genuinely infinite and there is always further in to go.

Progress Over Perfection

One of the greatest misunderstandings in the Christian life is expecting instant perfection. But the process is not about becoming flawless overnight. It is about moving forward, becoming more aligned, reflecting more of the original design over time.

Progress is evidence of the process working. The person who is living more patiently this year than last year, more honestly this year than last year, more free from some old compulsion this year than last year — that person is being transformed, whether or not they have fully arrived at the goal. And the goal, for all of us, is one we will not fully arrive at in this life. That is not a failure condition. It is the condition of every growing believer who has ever lived.

John is direct about this:

> *"If we claim to be without sin, we deceive ourselves and the truth is not in us. If we confess our sins, he is faithful and just and will forgive us our sins and purify us from all unrighteousness."*

– 1 John 1:8-9 (NIV)

A believer still sins. A believer who claims otherwise is self-deceived. But the provision is in place. Confession is met with forgiveness. Purification is ongoing. The relationship is secure, and the process continues. This is a realistic and tender picture of the Christian life, and it will free you from a perfectionism that the New Testament never required.

Setbacks Do Not Cancel the Rewrite

There will be moments when the old system appears to resurface. A pattern you thought was gone returns. A desire you thought was dead flares up. A reaction you thought you had outgrown catches you by surprise. These moments can be devastating. They can tempt you to wonder whether any real change has happened at all.

But setbacks do not mean the new code is gone. They do not mean the process has failed. They mean the override is still in progress. Setbacks are part of the rewriting cycle. The right response to a setback is not to panic and conclude that the whole project was a fantasy. The right response is to do what Scripture has always counseled: confess, receive forgiveness, return to the Spirit, and continue.

> *"for though the righteous fall seven times, they rise again, but the wicked stumble when calamity strikes."*
>
> **– Proverbs 24:16 (NIV)**

The mark of the righteous is not that they never fall. It is that they always rise. The mark of the transformation is not the absence of setbacks. It is the recovery from them. A tree that is being grown may lose leaves in a storm, but its roots are deeper after the storm than before, and its trunk is stronger. A believer who walks with the Spirit through setbacks emerges more rooted, more realistic, and more dependent on the One who is actually doing the work.

The Increasing Influence of the New Code

As the process continues, old patterns weaken. New patterns strengthen. Alignment becomes more consistent. Eventually, the system begins to default to the new nature.

This does not mean temptation disappears. It does not mean the flesh ceases to speak. It means the voice of the Spirit has become familiar enough, the new desires have grown strong enough, and the new habits have become automatic enough, that the old voice no longer controls the outputs even when it is still occasionally heard.

Paul describes the end point of this process in terms that almost take your breath:

> *"For those God foreknew he also predestined to be conformed to the image of his Son, that he might be the firstborn among many brothers and sisters."*
>
> **– Romans 8:29 (NIV)**

Conformed to the image of his Son. That is the destination. Not simply a better version of yourself, but an image-bearer increasingly marked with the likeness of Christ. This is what the Spirit is doing, every day, in every believer who will cooperate. And every year of a life lived in that cooperation moves the believer closer to that final likeness.

Living in the Tension

This stage of life is lived between two realities — what you were, and what you are becoming. The tension is real, but it is temporary. Because the direction is clear: toward restoration.

Many believers, at some point in the journey, learn to stop resisting the tension and start trusting it. The tension is not a sign of failure. It is a sign of movement. A completed structure has no tension in it; a cantilevered bridge being built has tension everywhere, because something is being held in a new position until the full structure can support it. Your life, as the Spirit forms you, is a bridge under construction. The tension is the evidence that the construction is actually happening.

Paul models this kind of trust as well as anyone:

> *"Not that I have already obtained all this, or have already arrived at my goal, but I press on to take hold of that for which Christ Jesus took hold of me. Brothers and sisters, I do not consider myself yet to have taken hold of it. But one thing I do: Forgetting what is behind and straining toward what is ahead, I press on toward the goal to win the prize for which God has called me heavenward in Christ Jesus."*
>
> **– Philippians 3:12-14 (NIV)**

Even Paul, late in his ministry, writes like a man who is still becoming. Not yet arrived. Still pressing on. Still straining forward. This is realistic, and it is freeing. If Paul is still in process, it is all right that you are, too.

Closing Thought

Transformation is not a single moment. It is a continuous process, in which the original design steadily overrides the corrupted code. And with time, what once felt unnatural becomes the way you live.

Do not despise the dailiness of this. The Spirit is not in a hurry because eternity is in view. Every ordinary day of cooperation with Him — every small moment of awareness, surrender, obedience, and return after setback — is contributing to a rewrite that will not be complete until Christ returns, but that is real, steady, and actually happening now.

CHAPTER 12

/ THREE LAYERS OF RESTORATION

Three Layers of Restoration

Justification, Regeneration, and Sanctification

Up to this point, we have explored how transformation happens — rebirth installs the new code, the Spirit governs the rewrite, and the process unfolds over time. Now we need to understand what is actually happening at every level. Because restoration is not one-dimensional. It operates in layers.

What God does in a person is not just a single process. It is a complete work across position, identity, and function. Three distinct but interwoven layers, each addressing a different aspect of the corrupted system, all executing simultaneously from the moment of rebirth onward.

Why This Matters

Many people misunderstand transformation because they only see one layer. Some focus exclusively on behavior. Some focus exclusively on identity. Some focus exclusively on spiritual experience. Each of those emphases has a piece of the truth, but any one of them in isolation produces a distorted picture of what God is actually doing.

If you miss the layers, you will misinterpret the process. You will panic about things you should relax about, and you will relax about things you should engage. You will mistake position for function, or function for position. You will either collapse into anxious self-effort or drift into passive presumption. You will evaluate your progress by the wrong instrument, and you will find yourself either too discouraged or too comfortable.

Theologians, working from the New Testament, have long named these three layers with specific terms: justification, regeneration, and sanctification. Each term addresses a different facet of what God does in the believer. None can be collapsed into the others. All belong together.

Layer 1: Justification — The Legal Reset

This is the first layer. It happens instantly.

At the moment of rebirth, something shifts in your position before God. Guilt is removed. Judgment is no longer held against you. Your standing is restored. This is not based on your performance. It is based on what has been done for you by Christ, and received by you through faith.

> *"for all have sinned and fall short of the glory of God, and all are justified freely by his grace through the redemption that came by Christ Jesus."*
>
> **– Romans 3:23-24 (NIV)**

Justified freely. The Greek word translated justified is dikaioo, a verdict-rendering word drawn from a courtroom. To justify is to declare legally righteous. Not to make a person righteous in their behavior — that is a different work — but to declare them righteous in their standing before the judge. Justification is a declaration about status, not a description of performance.

Paul elaborates this logic in Romans 5:

> *"Therefore, since we have been justified through faith, we have peace with God through our Lord Jesus Christ."*
>
> **– Romans 5:1 (NIV)**

Peace with God. Not a reduction of hostility, not a truce, not an ongoing negotiation. Peace. Because the legal matter has been settled. The case has been closed. The verdict has been rendered in favor of the one in Christ, and the basis of the verdict is the righteousness of Christ imputed to them, not the righteousness of their own behavior.

This is the doctrine that sparked the Protestant Reformation and has been the subject of millions of pages of theological discussion since. For our purposes, the essential point is simple. The legal dimension of your standing before God has been completely reset. Not being reset, gradually, as you improve. Reset — finished — at the moment of faith in Christ. This is not something that grows. This is something that is either true or not true. And for the person in Christ, it is true, now, fully.

What this means. Even while the rest of the system is still being rewritten, you are no longer defined by your past. You are no longer under condemnation. You are accepted at the highest level. Your position is restored before your behavior is perfected. This removes the pressure of trying to earn what has already been given.

> *"Therefore, there is now no condemnation for those who are in Christ Jesus."*
>
> **– Romans 8:1 (NIV)**

No condemnation. Now. Not after you have grown sufficiently. Now. This is load-bearing for everything else that happens in the Christian life. Transformation proceeds from a secure position, not toward one. The Father is not waiting for you to become good enough to receive His acceptance. His acceptance has already been given. The rest of the work is the unfolding of what that acceptance means in your actual life.

Layer 2: Regeneration — The New Core Installed

This is the second layer. It happens at the moment of rebirth, and its effects continue to unfold.

Regeneration is the installation of a new nature. The Spirit enters. The Source is reconnected. A new internal identity is established. This is the work we explored in Chapter 9. It is the architectural event — the reinstallation of the Original Source Code.

> *"he saved us, not because of righteous things we had done, but because of his mercy. He saved us through the washing of rebirth and renewal by the Holy Spirit."*
>
> **– Titus 3:5 (NIV)**

The washing of rebirth. A cleansing inaugural event. The renewal by the Holy Spirit. A fresh installation of divine life in the human being. At the deepest level, you are no longer operating from the same origin. Your desires begin to shift. Your internal direction begins to change. You are not just improving. You are becoming something new.

Peter, writing to his readers, speaks of regeneration in terms of new seed:

> *"Praise be to the God and Father of our Lord Jesus Christ! In his great mercy he has given us new birth into a living hope through the resurrection of Jesus Christ from the dead."*
>
> **– 1 Peter 1:3 (NIV)**

New birth into a living hope. The regeneration is linked, for Peter, to the resurrection of Jesus. The same power that raised Christ from death to life is the power that has raised the believer from spiritual death to spiritual life. The source layer has been re-energized by the very power that broke the tomb on Easter morning.

What this changes. Before, you were defined by a corrupted nature. After, you are defined by a restored connection to the Source. This is the foundation of transformation. Behavior flows from identity, and identity now flows from indwelling.

You are not trying to act like someone you are not. You are living out what you have actually become.

The Identity Shift

Between justification and the ongoing process of sanctification sits this second layer, regeneration — and it is, in some ways, the most misunderstood of the three. Justification is easy to grasp as a legal reset; sanctification is easy to grasp as an ongoing growth; regeneration, being a one-time installation of a new nature, is harder to see because it is internal and architectural.

But regeneration is where identity actually changes. Under justification alone, a believer might still think of himself as a sinner who has been legally forgiven. Under regeneration, a believer is invited to think of himself differently — as a new creation, indwelt by the Spirit of God, fundamentally changed at the source layer even if the operating system and hardware have not yet been fully renewed.

> *"Therefore, if anyone is in Christ, the new creation has come: The old has gone, the new is here!"*
>
> **– 2 Corinthians 5:17 (NIV)**

Paul does not describe the believer as an improved version of the old self. He describes the believer as a new creation. This is identity language. The believer's self-understanding is meant to begin here — not with the old labels inherited from a broken past, but with the new identity installed by the Spirit at rebirth.

This is why behavior flows from identity. If you believe your identity is "sinner working hard to become good," your behavior will be shaped by that. If you believe your identity is "new creation learning to live out who I actually am," your behavior will be shaped by that. Both of these are available labels in the New Testament, but Paul spends most of his energy insisting on the second one, because it is the one that tells the deeper truth.

Layer 3: Sanctification — The Ongoing Rewrite

This is the third layer. It is the process we explored in the previous chapter.

Sanctification is the continuous transformation of the system. Old patterns replaced. New patterns established. Alignment increasing over time. This is where the new position and the new identity begin to be worked out in the actual daily experience of the believer in the way they speak, decide, react, relate, work, suffer, and love.

> *"May God himself, the God of peace, sanctify you through and through. May your whole spirit, soul and body be kept blameless at the coming of our Lord Jesus Christ."*
>
> **– 1 Thessalonians 5:23 (NIV)**

Sanctify you through and through. Your whole spirit, soul, and body. This is the scope of sanctification. Not just the spiritual dimension. Every layer. The Spirit's rewrite is not restricted to religious behavior or inner piety. It touches every area of life, progressively, as the process unfolds.

What this looks like. Growth in consistency. Decrease in internal conflict. Increasing alignment between identity and action. This is where the system begins to reflect the Original Design again — not perfectly, not uniformly, but increasingly, over time, as the Spirit's work deepens.

How the Layers Work Together

These three layers are not separate. They are connected. Justification secures your position. Regeneration establishes your identity. Sanctification transforms your function.

Together, they create a complete picture. You are accepted. You are made new. You are being transformed. None of these can be collapsed into either of the others. Justification without regeneration would be a legal reset without an internal change—a person declared righteous but unchanged at the source. That is not the biblical picture. God does not merely acquit the guilty; He remakes them.

Regeneration without sanctification would be an internal change that never shows up in the actual life of the believer — a new nature installed but never expressed in observable living. That is also not the biblical picture. The Spirit who is installed is not inactive; He is at work, and His work becomes visible.

Sanctification without justification and regeneration would be moral effort without a foundation — a person trying to build a better life on unsettled standing and unchanged nature. That would be the religious performance we have already described as impossible. Without justification, there is no peace. Without regeneration, there is no capacity. Sanctification, severed from the first two layers, is just the old exhausted effort under a new name.

Why People Get Confused

Confusion happens when one layer is isolated from the others. If you focus only on justification, you may ignore transformation. You may live with a theological confidence in your legal standing while showing little evidence of actual change in how you live. This is a real danger. James pointedly warns against a faith that produces no corresponding works, calling such a faith dead.

If you focus only on sanctification, you may fall into performance. You may treat the Christian life as a rigorous self-improvement project, measuring your worth before God by how well you are doing this week. This leaves you oscillating between pride when you are doing well and despair when you are not. Both are evidence that justification has slipped out of view.

If you focus only on regeneration, you may miss the ongoing process. You may treat your initial experience of rebirth as if it were the whole story, and neglect the actual daily work of cooperation with the Spirit that is the shape of real growth over time.

Balance is essential. Each layer is protected by the other two. Your position before God is secured by justification; therefore you can grow without anxiety. Your identity has been renewed by regeneration; therefore you actually can grow. Your function is being transformed by sanctification; therefore growth is what the Christian life actually looks like over time.

The Confidence This Creates

When you understand the layers, you do not panic when you are still growing. You do not rely on performance for acceptance. You trust the process without losing perspective.

You know your position is secure. You know your identity is established. You know your transformation is in progress. These three knowings, held together, produce a particular kind of stability that is hard to shake — not because your feelings are constant, but because your theology is aligned with reality.

> *"And those he predestined, he also called; those he called, he also justified; those he justified, he also glorified."*
>
> **– Romans 8:30 (NIV)**

Paul ends this chain with a past-tense verb that is still astonishing: he also glorified. The whole sequence, including the end, is described as already accomplished in the mind of God. From justification at the beginning to glorification at the end, the story is settled. What remains is for the story to unfold in your actual experience. But the outcome is not in doubt.

A Helpful Way to Hold It

If it helps, think of the three layers this way. Justification is the verdict. Regeneration is the birth. Sanctification is the growing up. Together, these three layers form the complete Restoration Protocol — God's comprehensive answer to every dimension of what the breach damaged.

Justification — the verdict. A declaration made about you, rendering you legally righteous in Christ. Instant, complete, unchanging. Regeneration — the birth. An event that happens to you, installing a new nature and the indwelling Spirit. Instant, complete in principle, unfolding in expression.

Sanctification — the growing up. A process that continues throughout your life, as the new nature increasingly governs the operating system and the body. Ongoing, progressive, and not finished until the day of Christ.

Each of the three describes a real action of God in the believer. None of them can be performed by the believer. All three arrive as gifts and take effect through faith. Together, they constitute what Scripture means when it speaks of salvation — a salvation that is, in one sense, accomplished once for all at the cross and the empty tomb, and in another sense, being worked out in the believer every day of his life until the day when it is fully and finally complete.

Closing Thought

God is not doing one thing in you. He is doing three things at once: restoring your standing, recreating your nature, and rewriting your life.

All of it is moving you toward full alignment with the Original Source Code. Not some of the way. All of the way. And the fact that you are still in process is not evidence that God is finished or absent. It is evidence that He is still at work —

patient, thorough, and entirely committed to completing what He began.

CHAPTER

13

/ FALSE FIXES

False Fixes

Why External Solutions Cannot Heal an Internal Corruption

When a system malfunctions, the instinct of every user is the same: find a fix. Reboot the device. Reinstall the application. Replace the hardware. Download a patch. The malfunction demands a solution, and a solution must be supplied. This instinct, in its general shape, is not wrong. It is, in fact, a residual memory of design—humanity knows, beneath all the noise, that it was made to run, and that it is not running correctly.

Something inside every human being is still calling out for restoration. The ache of the world is, in part, the ache of a creature that remembers it was once whole and now is not. But if the instinct is sound, the execution is almost universally flawed, because humanity keeps trying to repair an internal problem with external tools.

The Original Source Code is not a surface application that can be re-downloaded from a server; it is the core program written into the spirit by the breath of God. When that core is corrupted, no outside fix will reach it. Every human attempt to restore the system from outside the system is, in the end, a false fix—an intervention that may temporarily mask the symptoms but cannot address the virus at the root.

Scripture treats this tendency with almost exhausted clarity. Again and again the human heart is described as reaching for remedies that cannot reach where the wound lies. The prophet Jeremiah records the Lord lamenting, "My people have committed two sins: they have forsaken me, the spring of living water, and have dug their own cisterns, broken cisterns that cannot hold water" (Jeremiah 2:13). The image is devastating in its precision. A cistern is a human construction designed to store water. But a broken cistern leaks. What the prophet describes is not merely the choice of a lesser water source; it is the choice of a lesser water source that will not even hold the water that is poured into it. Humanity, cut off from the Source, keeps digging fixes that cannot retain the life they are supposed to supply.

The self-help book works for a season, then empties. The new relationship soothes for a time, then leaks. The promotion satisfies for a quarter, then runs dry. Each cistern promises to solve the thirst, and each cistern loses the water. The problem is not that humans are stupid; it is that a spirit cut off from its Source has no other option but to try to manufacture life from materials that cannot produce life.

> *"My people have committed two sins: They have forsaken me, the spring of living water, and have dug their own cisterns, broken cisterns that cannot hold water."*
>
> **– Jeremiah 2:13 (NIV)**

This chapter examines the most common categories of false fixes that humanity has manufactured in response to its malfunction. Self-help and the illusion of self-rewrite. Success and the pursuit of achievement without alignment. Pleasure and the temporary override of discomfort. Identity construction without a Source. And perhaps most tragic of all, religion without transformation—a counterfeit restoration that wears the language of the real fix but leaves the code untouched.

Each of these approaches has helped in some surface way; each has produced real short-term change in the lives of real people; and each has, in the end, proved incapable of reaching the actual break. To see why will not only clarify the gospel of the Source; it will also liberate those who have exhausted themselves trying fixes that were never designed to work.

Self-Help: The Illusion That the Corrupted Can Rewrite Itself

The first and most popular false fix in the modern age is self-help. Its logic is simple: the human being is broken, the human being has power, therefore the human being can repair the human being. This logic is so assumed in contemporary culture that to question it can feel like heresy. An entire industry has been built on the premise.

Libraries of books promise the reader seven habits, twelve steps, five rules, four agreements, one morning routine that will transform the life into what it should be. The premise of this industry is that the tools for repair reside within the self and need only to be properly accessed, organized, and applied. The malfunctioning system, it is said, can rewrite its own code.

The premise is, from a biblical standpoint, a theological impossibility. Scripture does not teach that the human spirit is partially damaged and can repair itself with effort. It teaches that the human spirit is dead in its relationship to God and therefore cannot, of itself, generate the life it has lost. Paul writes, "As for you, you were dead in your transgressions and sins" (Ephesians 2:1). Dead systems do not reboot themselves. A body in the grave does not decide, one morning, to rise. The corpse cannot work up the energy required to live. What Ephesians 2 announces in the verses that follow is not that the dead organized themselves into resurrection, but that "God, who is rich in mercy, made us alive with Christ even when we were dead in transgressions" (Ephesians 2:4-5). Life comes from outside the dead. Self-help asks a corpse to lift itself, and when it fails, it tells the corpse to try harder next quarter.

> *"As for you, you were dead in your transgressions and sins... But because of his great love for us, God, who is rich in mercy, made us alive with Christ even when we were dead in transgressions—it is by grace you have been saved."*
>
> **– Ephesians 2:1,4-5 (NIV)**

There is a real, narrower truth that self-help accidentally brushes against. Human beings were created with genuine agency—a will that can cooperate with life or resist it, a mind that can be trained, habits that can be formed. The Proverbs are full of disciplines the wise person adopts rising early, guarding the tongue, avoiding foolish companions, working diligently.

Scripture absolutely values the cultivation of habits and the shaping of character. But the Proverbs never teach that these disciplines, practiced in isolation from the Lord, can regenerate a spirit that is dead. They are fruit, not root. Self-help, cut off from the Source, attempts to grow fruit on a tree that has been severed at the trunk. For a time, the stored sap will produce leaves. Given months or years, the tree will wither, because no discipline can reconnect the branch to the vine that has been broken.

Jesus speaks directly to this in the vine metaphor: "I am the vine; you are the branches. If you remain in me and I in you, you will bear much fruit; apart from me you can do nothing" (John 15:5). The language is absolute. "Apart from me you can do nothing." Not "you can do less." Not "you can do mediocre." Nothing—no enduring, Source-bearing fruit.

A self-help practice can produce external fruit that looks like the real thing, for a season, and then withers because it was never connected to the vine. The sober man whose sobriety was willed, not restored, relapses. The disciplined woman whose discipline was a performance, not a transformation, burns out.

The spiritual seeker whose spirituality was curated, not indwelt, grows tired. The branch, cut off, cannot sustain itself forever on stored sap.

> *"I am the vine; you are the branches. If you remain in me and I in you, you will bear much fruit; apart from me you can do nothing."*
>
> **– John 15:5 (NIV)**

There is a further, more insidious danger in self-help as a false fix: it trains the soul to trust itself rather than the Source. Each incremental improvement, achieved by will, can strengthen the conviction that the self is the solution. And a soul that believes itself to be the solution is a soul progressively sealed against the real Solution.

The person who has "gotten their life together" through discipline can find it harder to receive the gospel than the person whose life is visibly falling apart, because the first has evidence that the flesh can perform and the second has no such evidence. Jesus often found deeper receptivity in the broken than in the accomplished, not because brokenness is holy but because brokenness has stopped pretending that self-help was working.

Success: Achievement Without Alignment

The second false fix is success, which is self-help's older and wealthier cousin. Where self-help aims at the improvement of the internal self, success aims at the accumulation of external outcomes—wealth, status, accomplishment, recognition, influence. The premise of success as a fix is that the malfunction inside will go silent when the life outside is impressive enough. Build the career. Earn the title. Acquire the house. Win the award. Accumulate enough of the world's marks of arrival, and the ache will finally fall silent. This, too, is a theological error, because it attempts to address a spiritual problem with material inputs. The spirit does not eat status; it was designed to be fed by God.

No book of Scripture dismantles this fix more ruthlessly than Ecclesiastes. The Preacher—traditionally identified with Solomon, a man with the resources to run every experiment—tests success in all its forms. He tries pleasure: “I denied myself nothing my eyes desired” (Ecclesiastes 2:10). He tries achievement: “I undertook great projects: I built houses for myself and planted vineyards. I made gardens and parks and planted all kinds of fruit trees in them. I made reservoirs... I became greater by far than anyone in Jerusalem before me” (Ecclesiastes 2:4-9).

He tries wisdom, wealth, work, and reputation. And then, at the end of each experiment, he records the same verdict, with a kind of bone-tired honesty: “Yet when I surveyed all that my hands had done and what I had toiled to achieve, everything was meaningless, a chasing after the wind; nothing was gained under the sun” (Ecclesiastes 2:11).

> *“I denied myself nothing my eyes desired; I refused my heart no pleasure... Yet when I surveyed all that my hands had done and what I had toiled to achieve, everything was meaningless, a chasing after the wind; nothing was gained under the sun.”*
>
> **– Ecclesiastes 2:10-11 (NIV)**

The Hebrew word rendered “meaningless” is **hevel**, which literally means vapor, breath, a puff of air that vanishes when grasped. The Preacher is not saying that gardens and vineyards are evil; he is saying that they cannot hold the weight he tried to place on them. He wanted success to feed his spirit, and success is not spiritual food. It is vapor—visible, even beautiful, but weightless when held and gone when the hand closes. This is why the person who finally attains what they were chasing often discovers a strange depression on the other side of the attainment. The promotion arrives and the ache has not moved. The book becomes a bestseller and the emptiness is still present at breakfast. The house is bought and the soul is not yet home.

Jesus spoke of this directly when He asked, "What good will it be for someone to gain the whole world, yet forfeit their soul?" (Matthew 16:26). The question is not merely rhetorical; it is diagnostic. Jesus assumes that soul and world operate on different currencies. One cannot be purchased with the other.

A soul disconnected from God cannot be fed on worldly currency, no matter how much of that currency is accumulated, because soul-hunger is not a resource shortage but a connection failure. The Preacher's despair and Jesus's question land in the same place: success, detached from the Source, is a counterfeit food that cannot nourish a spirit that has been designed to live on something else.

> *"What good will it be for someone to gain the whole world, yet forfeit their soul? Or what can anyone give in exchange for their soul?"*
>
> **– Matthew 16:26 (NIV)**

Perhaps the most painful testimony to this truth is the frequency with which outwardly successful people report inward collapse. The Preacher's conclusion is repeated in a thousand contemporary biographies. The performer at the top of their field struggles with depression. The entrepreneur who built the empire cannot sleep at night. The celebrity universally admired is privately medicated. Not because success is cursed, but because success was never designed to play the role they asked it to play. It was designed to be a fruit of alignment, not a substitute for it. Used as ornament it can be good; used as substitute it always fails.

It is worth saying here, because the reader may have felt the critique above as a blanket dismissal of success itself, that this is not what Scripture teaches and not what this chapter intends. Success, properly understood and properly ordered, is a good thing. It is a fruit of diligence, wisdom, faithfulness, and the favor of God. What Scripture—and this book—reject is success severed from its source, asked to do the work that only the Source can do. I have explored the positive, integrated shape of success at length in my earlier book,

Success, The Total Package, which attempts to show what it looks like when achievement, relationships, character, purpose, and spirit are working together rather than at cross-purposes. The burden of that book is that success becomes life-giving only when it is a byproduct of a whole person running in alignment; the burden of this chapter is the complementary warning that success, when asked to be the center, becomes one of the most sophisticated false fixes humanity has ever devised. The two messages are two sides of the same truth: success cannot save you, but when you are saved, success can be restored to its proper place as fruit rather than idol.

Pleasure: The Anesthetic That Wears Off

The third false fix is pleasure. Where self-help attempts to repair the system and success attempts to compensate for the malfunction with external accumulation, pleasure attempts to silence the malfunction with sensory input. The fix here is simpler and more honest than the others: it does not promise to repair anything; it only promises to make the malfunction feel, for a while, less painful. Alcohol, food, sexual immorality, entertainment, shopping, drugs, scrolling, gambling, stimulation of every kind—each plays the role of anesthetic. Each raises the dopamine in the moment, and each leaves the system, when the anesthetic wears off, more worn than before.

Scripture is not ascetic; it does not treat pleasure as evil in itself. The Psalms celebrate wine that "gladdens human hearts" (Psalm 104:15). The Song of Songs celebrates sexual intimacy within marriage. The festivals of Israel included feasting and music and dancing. God is the author of pleasure, not its enemy. What Scripture consistently warns against is the use of pleasure as a substitute for God—the demand that sensory input do the work that only communion with the Source can do. Paul writes of those whose "god is their stomach, and their glory is in their shame. Their mind is set on earthly things" (Philippians 3:19). The stomach-god is not the stomach; it is the stomach put in the place of God. The problem is not the appetite; it is the enthronement of the appetite.

> *"Their destiny is destruction, their god is their stomach, and their glory is in their shame. Their mind is set on earthly things."*
>
> **– Philippians 3:19 (NIV)**

Pleasure as anesthetic follows a predictable pattern, often called the law of diminishing returns. The first drink silences the ache more than the next. The first binge of entertainment satisfies more than the next. The tenth satisfies less than the first and the hundredth satisfies less than the tenth.

The system is being asked to solve a spiritual problem with a sensory signal, and the sensory signal keeps needing to be stronger to produce the same silencing. This is the architecture of addiction. It is why the addict does not, at a certain point, even enjoy the substance; the substance has ceased to give pleasure and now only prevents pain. The anesthetic is no longer a luxury but a necessity; without it, the untreated ache is unbearable. The addict is not enjoying the anesthetic; the addict is avoiding the wound.

The writer of Hebrews notes with characteristic candor that sin offers "the fleeting pleasures of sin" (Hebrews 11:25). The word fleeting is not a moralistic scold; it is a technical description. The pleasures really are pleasures—Scripture does not deny this. And they really are fleeting—Scripture does not romanticize this either. The dopamine fires and the dopamine falls, and when the dopamine falls the ache returns with interest, because the underlying system has not been repaired, only deferred. Pleasure as fix is a loan against a future the spirit cannot pay. Every anesthetic bill eventually comes due, and the cost of the delay is higher than the cost of facing the wound directly would have been.

> *"He chose to be mistreated along with the people of God rather than to enjoy the fleeting pleasures of sin."*
>
> **– Hebrews 11:25 (NIV)**

The Samaritan woman at the well is a living image of pleasure as false fix. She had been through five husbands, and the man she was now with was not her husband (John 4:18). The geometry of her life suggests a woman trying to fix an internal thirst with the external presence of another person, and each person failing to be the fix. Jesus does not lecture her about her relationships; He diagnoses the system underneath. "Everyone who drinks this water will be thirsty again, but whoever drinks the water I give them will never thirst" (John 4:13-14). The water that fails to satisfy is not condemned; it is simply identified as water that cannot do what she is asking it to do. Jesus offers a different water, and He offers it without moralizing. He does not say she is bad for being thirsty; He says she is looking in the wrong place.

Identity Construction: Defining the Self Without the Source

The fourth false fix is newer in its contemporary form but ancient in its root. It is the attempt to solve the malfunction of the spirit by constructing an identity from within the self, without reference to the Source. The premise is that if the self can sufficiently define itself—choose its labels, declare its truth, narrate its story—the malfunction will be silenced by the coherence of the self-construction. The language of this fix fills the modern vocabulary: authenticity, self-actualization, self-definition, living your truth, finding yourself. In each phrase, the self is both the builder and the building, the designer and the design. The corrupted code is asked to produce a coherent identity without access to the Source that first defined it.

Scripture, from the very first chapter, locates identity in the Creator, not in the creature. Humanity is made "in the image of God" (Genesis 1:27). The image comes first; the imaged being second. The identity of humanity is not self-generated but conferred. To attempt to construct identity without reference to the One whose image the human being bears is, theologically, to attempt to build a mirror while denying the existence of a face.

The mirror can reflect many shapes, but without a face it reflects none of them truly. Identity constructed without the Source will always be unstable, because the one doing the constructing is himself unfinished; he is both the sculptor and the marble, and no sculptor carves himself into permanence using his own hands.

> *"So God created mankind in his own image, in the image of God he created them; male and female he created them."*
>
> **– Genesis 1:27 (NIV)**

The book of Judges records a recurring formula that captures the logic of self-constructed identity: "In those days Israel had no king; everyone did as they saw fit" (Judges 21:25). The clause translated "as they saw fit" reads more literally in Hebrew as "what was right in his own eyes." Each person, cut off from a shared source of definition, defines rightness by reference to himself. The result, in Judges, is not freedom but chaos.

Everyone has their own truth, and the collisions of those truths produce violence, idolatry, and fragmentation. The modern experiment in self-constructed identity is producing a strikingly similar social texture. Where there is no source outside the self, every self becomes its own standard, and every collision becomes existentially intolerable, because to disagree with another's self-construction is to threaten their only source of stability.

The deeper problem with self-constructed identity is spiritual. The self, as the soul knows at the level it does not speak aloud, is not whole. It is corrupted. It carries, as previous chapters have shown, an inherited virus. To ask the corrupted self to generate its own definition is to ask a damaged camera to produce an accurate photograph of itself using its own damaged sensor. Whatever image emerges will carry the distortion built into the instrument.

The biblical alternative is not to repress the self but to receive a definition that comes from outside the damaged instrument. Paul writes of the believer: "For you died, and your life is now hidden with Christ in God" (Colossians 3:3). The new identity is not fabricated; it is received. It is not built by the self; it is hidden in God and revealed through Christ. The self, finally, is known not by looking into itself, but by looking into the One whose image it bears.

> *"For you died, and your life is now hidden with Christ in God."*
>
> **– Colossians 3:3 (NIV)**

Religion Without Transformation: The Counterfeit Fix

The fifth and most tragic false fix is religion without transformation. It is the most tragic because it wears the language of the real fix while leaving the actual malfunction untouched. A person can spend a lifetime in church services, doctrinal study, ethical performance, ritual observance, tithing, community involvement, and even Christian vocation, and remain untouched by the regeneration that the Source Code requires. Such a person has absorbed the vocabulary of restoration without ever receiving the restoration itself. Religion without transformation is the most dangerous false fix because the religious person does not even know that the fix has failed; the external activity masks the unchanged interior so thoroughly that diagnosis becomes almost impossible.

Jesus spoke about this fix more directly and more often than about any of the others. Quoting Isaiah, He said of the religious leaders of His day: "These people honor me with their lips, but their hearts are far from me. They worship me in vain" (Matthew 15:8-9; cf. Isaiah 29:13). The diagnosis is surgical. The mouth is present; the heart is not. The external activity is occurring; the internal condition is unchanged. The malfunction has not been fixed; it has been dressed. Later, He said to the Pharisees—the most religious men of their generation—"You are like whitewashed tombs, which look beautiful on the outside but on the inside are full of the bones of the dead and everything unclean" (Matthew 23:27). The tomb is ornamented; the corpse inside has not been resurrected. This is religion without transformation, and Jesus reserved His sharpest words for it, not because He despised religion, but because He despised the counterfeit that prevented people from seeking the real cure.

> *"These people honor me with their lips, but their hearts are far from me. They worship me in vain; their teachings are merely human rules."*
>
> **– Matthew 15:8-9 (NIV)**

Paul adds his own warning to those who would rely on religion as a fix. He writes that in the last days people will be "having a form of godliness but denying its power" (2 Timothy 3:5). The phrase "form of godliness" describes the external shape; the "power" is the transforming operation of the Holy Spirit inside. A person can retain the form while losing—or never receiving—the power. The form includes the right vocabulary, the right associations, the right behavioral markers. The power is the active, indwelling presence of the Spirit rewriting the code from within. To have the form without the power is to be religious and unregenerate, which is the exact condition Jesus diagnoses in the Pharisees.

> *"Having a form of godliness but denying its power. Have nothing to do with such people."*
>
> **– 2 Timothy 3:5 (NIV)**

Colossians gives yet another angle on this counterfeit fix. Paul warns against submission to rules that "have indeed an appearance of wisdom, with their self-imposed worship, their false humility and their harsh treatment of the body, but they lack any value in restraining sensual indulgence" (Colossians 2:23). He is describing a religious program that adds layer upon layer of rule, discipline, and restriction—a program that looks wise, even severe—and that nonetheless lacks the actual power to change the inner person.

The person under such a program can appear more controlled without being more transformed. The same malfunction runs underneath; only the external appearance has been rearranged. Colossians is not condemning discipline; it is condemning discipline that substitutes for union with Christ, which alone has the power to rewrite the interior.

How does one know whether one's religion is the real thing or the counterfeit? Scripture offers a consistent test: fruit. "By their fruit you will recognize them," Jesus said (Matthew 7:20). Not their vocabulary. Not their attendance. Not their theological precision. Their fruit—the slow, actual, observable output of the inner system over time. The fruits of the Spirit, which Galatians 5 lists as love, joy, peace, patience, kindness, goodness, faithfulness, gentleness, and self-control, are not simply behaviors that religious people can perform on their best days; they are the signature output of a spirit indwelt by the Holy Spirit over the long arc of a life. Where the fruit is missing across years of religious performance, there is strong reason to suspect that the form of godliness is present without the power—that the system is dressed but not restored.

> *"Thus, by their fruit you will recognize them."*
>
> **– Matthew 7:20 (NIV)**

Why Every False Fix Shares the Same Architecture

It is worth noting, at the end of this chapter, that every false fix surveyed above shares a single underlying architecture. Each one attempts to address an internal, spiritual malfunction with a resource that exists outside the spirit. Self-help uses will. Success uses accumulation. Pleasure uses sensation. Identity construction uses narrative. Religion without transformation uses performance.

Each of these resources is good in its own right and has its own proper place. But none of them can reach the place where the real problem lives. The Original Source Code is written into the spirit, not the will, the environment, the senses, the narrative, or the performance. Only a resource that can reach the spirit can repair the spirit, and the only resource that can reach the spirit is the Spirit of God.

This is why the gospel is, at its core, not another self-help program but an announcement that the Source has come to us. Jesus did not arrive teaching a new technique by which the corrupted could repair themselves. He arrived as the Source in human flesh, bearing in His own person the restoration that the human being could not generate. He did not say, "Try harder." He said, "Come to me, all you who are weary and burdened, and I will give you rest" (Matthew 11:28). He did not say, "Clean yourself up and then I will receive you." He said, "It is not the healthy who need a doctor, but the sick" (Mark 2:17). The gospel is a physician entering a ward of patients who have spent themselves on remedies that could not heal, and offering them the only cure that can.

> *"Come to me, all you who are weary and burdened, and I will give you rest. Take my yoke upon you and learn from me, for I am gentle and humble in heart, and you will find rest for your souls."*
>
> **– Matthew 11:28-30 (NIV)**

The reader who has spent years in false fixes may be discouraged by this chapter. That discouragement, if it arises, is actually the first sign of hope. The despair of the failed fix is often the threshold of the real one. The Preacher's "meaningless, meaningless" is not the end of Ecclesiastes; it is the doorway into the Preacher's final counsel: "Now all has been heard; here is the conclusion of the matter: Fear God and keep his commandments, for this is the duty of all mankind" (Ecclesiastes 12:13). The exhaustion of vapor-fixes prepares the soul for the real water.

When self-help has failed, success has hollowed, pleasure has worn thin, identity has fractured, and religion has revealed itself to be a form without power, the soul is finally, painfully, grace-fully positioned to hear what Jesus said to the woman at the well: there is a water that does not run dry. The false fixes will tell you it is inside you already, if only you could find it. The gospel says it is outside you, offered to you, waiting to be received.

> *"Now all has been heard; here is the conclusion of the matter: Fear God and keep his commandments, for this is the duty of all mankind."*
>
> **– Ecclesiastes 12:13 (NIV)**

The next chapter turns from the fixes that do not work to the life that does. It will describe, in practical detail, what it looks like to run restored—to be a human being whose Source

Code has been re-authored by the Holy Spirit, whose operating system is being rewritten by sanctification, and whose hardware is being re-purposed as a temple of the Living God. The false fixes have been named, not to shame the reader but to clear the ground. Nothing can be rebuilt on broken cisterns. But once the broken cisterns have been acknowledged, the spring of living water is not far away.

CHAPTER 14

/ RUNNING RESTORED

Running Restored

The Life of a System in Alignment with Its Source

The chapters to this point have traced a long arc: the original build of humanity as a system designed to run on the breath of God, the entry of the virus that corrupted the code, the failed human attempts at repair, and the divine intervention by which the Holy Spirit overwrites the corrupted spirit and begins the slow, continuous restoration of the whole person.

What remains is to describe, in practical and pastoral terms, what it actually looks like for a human being to run in this restored state. This is the chapter in which theology becomes life. The doctrines of regeneration and sanctification are not meant to sit in a textbook; they are meant to produce a particular kind of person in a particular kind of world. The question this chapter answers is deceptively simple: when the Source Code has been re-authored by the Holy Spirit, how does the restored system function day by day?

It is important to say at the outset that running restored does not mean running perfectly. Paul himself, writing to the most mature churches, repeatedly reminded his readers that they were still becoming, not yet arrived. "Not that I have already obtained all this, or have already arrived at my goal, but I press on to take hold of that for which Christ Jesus took hold of me" (Philippians 3:12).

The restored life is not the sinless life; it is the life that is progressively being conformed to Christ, whose direction has been reversed at the spiritual core, and whose fruit over time begins to look unmistakably like the character of the Spirit who indwells it. The pages that follow describe this kind of life, not as a romanticized ideal but as a realistic trajectory, acknowledging both the glory of what begins now and the imperfection that continues until the final resurrection.

> *"Not that I have already obtained all this, or have already arrived at my goal, but I press on to take hold of that for which Christ Jesus took hold of me."*
>
> **– Philippians 3:12 (NIV)**

The Language of the Source Code Is Love

Before we name any mark of the restored life, we must name the substance of the restored life. Because the restored system is not a list of behaviors. It is not a grid of disciplines. It is not an ethical performance assembled out of scattered virtues. Underneath every mark that will follow in this chapter, there is one substance, and that substance has a name. The language of the Source Code is love. This is not a poetic flourish. It is a structural claim. If the Source Code was originally written by God, and God is love (1 John 4:8), then love is not merely one output of the restored system.

Love is the native language in which the code is written. Every other function of the restored life is a dialect of it. Every fruit of the Spirit is a syllable of it. Every restored relationship, every healed voice, every reoriented desire, every restored vocation is love expressing itself in a particular grammar. Love is not a piece of the restoration. Love is the whole restoration, translated into a thousand scenarios.

> *"Whoever does not love does not know God, because God is love."*
>
> **– 1 John 4:8 (NIV)**

> *"And so we know and rely on the love God has for us. God is love. Whoever lives in love lives in God, and God in them."*
>
> **– 1 John 4:16 (NIV)**

The reason this must be said at the head of this chapter, and not at the end, is that the human mind—particularly the mind trained by religion—tends to read a list of virtues and file them as tasks. The restored person begins the list, works down to item four or five, and burns out. He has missed the architecture. Love is not one task among many; love is the operating principle underneath the whole list. When love is the substance, everything else flows. When love is absent, everything else stalls, no matter how polished the external performance looks.

Paul's Diagnosis: Without Love, the Code Is Unreadable

Paul makes this point so pointedly in 1 Corinthians 13 that it reshapes the entire Christian vocabulary. "If I speak in the tongues of men or of angels, but do not have love,

I am only a resounding gong or a clanging cymbal. If I have the gift of prophecy and can fathom all mysteries and all knowledge, and if I have a faith that can move mountains, but do not have love, I am nothing. If I give all I possess to the poor and give over my body to hardship that I may boast, but do not have love, I gain nothing" (1 Corinthians 13:1-3). Read that passage slowly. Paul lists the highest possible religious outputs—tongues of angels, prophecy, complete knowledge, mountain-moving faith, radical generosity, physical sacrifice—and then runs them all through the same filter. Without love, each one of them produces nothing. Not a little. Nothing. The implication is staggering: the gifts, disciplines, and sacrifices of religion can be performed without love, and when they are, the system produces noise, not code. A gong. A cymbal. A blank read-out.

> *"If I speak in the tongues of men or of angels, but do not have love, I am only a resounding gong or a clanging cymbal. If I have the gift of prophecy and can fathom all mysteries and all knowledge, and if I have a faith that can move mountains, but do not have love, I am nothing. If I give all I possess to the poor and give over my body to hardship that I may boast, but do not have love, I gain nothing."*

– 1 Corinthians 13:1-3 (NIV)

If love is not merely an output but the substance that gives every other output its meaning, then the restored system is not primarily about doing more good things. It is about being resourced in love, so that the good things that follow carry the signal they were designed to carry. The same sermon preached out of love lands differently from the same sermon preached out of duty. The same gift given out of love weighs differently in the hand of the receiver from the same gift given out of obligation. The same forgiveness extended out of love heals differently from the same words recited out of protocol. The code looks the same on the outside; inside, love is what makes it readable.

The Two Commandments Are One Grammar

When Jesus was asked which commandment was the greatest, He did not pick one from ten. He collapsed the whole law into two: "Love the Lord your God with all your heart and with all your soul and with all your mind and with all your strength. The second is this: Love your neighbor as yourself. There is no commandment greater than these" (Mark 12:30-31). And then, in Matthew's parallel, He adds a sentence that functions like a compiler instruction: "All the Law and the Prophets hang on these two commandments"

(Matthew 22:40). Hang. Every other commandment is dependent on these two. The Ten Commandments. The laws of

Leviticus. The words of the Prophets. The ethical commands of the Gospels and Epistles. Every single one of them is a specific, situational expression of the two great commandments, which are themselves two expressions of one reality: love. Love of God running vertically, love of neighbor running horizontally—the cross-shape of the code made from a single substance.

> *"Love the Lord your God with all your heart and with all your soul and with all your mind and with all your strength. The second is this: Love your neighbor as yourself. There is no commandment greater than these."*
>
> **– Mark 12:30-31 (NIV)**

> *"Love does no harm to a neighbor. Therefore love is the fulfillment of the law."*
>
> **– Romans 13:10 (NIV)**

Paul draws the same conclusion in Romans 13:10: "Love is the fulfillment of the law." Not the replacement. The fulfillment. The law was always pointing at love; love is what the law was always trying to produce. When love is running as the substance of the restored system, every letter of the law is being obeyed from the inside, because love is what obedience is made of. This explains why the earliest Christians could be described in a sentence: they loved. Tertullian, writing about how the watching Roman world perceived the first believers, captured the observation in a single famous line: "See how they love one another." That was not marketing. That was diagnosis. A new code was running in human beings, and its signature was visible at a glance.

The Source's Signature

Jesus was direct about this: love is the mark by which the restored community is recognized. "A new command I give you: Love one another. As I have loved you, so you must love one another. By this everyone will know that you are my disciples, if you love one another" (John 13:34-35). Notice what Jesus does not say. He does not say, "By your doctrinal precision everyone will know." He does not say, "By your moral strictness everyone will know." He does not say, "By your attendance records, your church buildings, your religious vocabulary, or your political stances." He says, "By your love." Because love is the Source's own signature, and a system carrying the Source's signature will be recognized by whoever is paying attention.

> *"A new command I give you: Love one another. As I have loved you, so you must love one another. By this everyone will know that you are my disciples, if you love one another."*
>
> **– John 13:34-35 (NIV)**

This is why, when John—writing perhaps fifty years after the resurrection, after a lifetime of watching the church grow and falter—reduces the whole of Christian experience to a diagnostic test, the test is love. "Dear friends, let us love one another, for love comes from God. Everyone who loves has been born of God and knows God. Whoever does not love does not know God, because God is love" (1 John 4:7-8). The test is not, "Have you experienced the right feelings?" The test is not, "Have you said the right words?" The test is, "Has love been planted in you and started to grow?" Because love comes from God; it cannot be manufactured by the corrupted system. If it is present, the Source is present. If it is absent, however impressive the religious activity, the Source has not yet arrived.

> *"Dear friends, let us love one another, for love comes from God. Everyone who loves has been born of God and knows God. Whoever does not love does not know God, because God is love."*
>
> **– 1 John 4:7-8 (NIV)**

What This Means for the Rest of This Chapter

Everything that follows in this chapter—peace, reoriented desire, renewed mind, redirected body, healed interface, restored relationships, reclaimed vocation, expanded horizon, restored voice, stable center, restored community—should be read as love speaking in different registers. Peace is love at rest. Reoriented desire is love choosing what it loves. The renewed mind is love thinking. The redirected body is love moving. Restored relationships are love between persons. Reclaimed vocation is love working. An expanded horizon is love remembering eternity. A restored voice is love speaking. A stable center is love standing. A restored community is love in the plural. Strip love out of any of these and the word remains, but the substance is gone.

Keep love at the center, and the marks that follow are simply love specifying itself for a thousand occasions. That is why this section had to come first. The language of the Source Code is love. Everything else in this chapter is its dialect.

A Reordered Interior: Peace as the Default State

The most immediate and often most surprising mark of a restored system is a reordered interior. Before regeneration, the inner world of the human being runs on a low-grade but persistent noise—a background anxiety that something is not right, a restlessness that the soul cannot name, a discontent that no external condition can fully silence.

Augustine wrote of this in the most famous line of his Confessions: "You have made us for yourself, O Lord, and our heart is restless until it rests in you." The restoration of the Source Code does not eliminate circumstantial stress; life still contains loss, illness, conflict, and uncertainty. What it does eliminate—or at least progressively reduce—is the deeper, architectural restlessness beneath the circumstances. Peace becomes the default state of the inner room, even when storms are occurring in the outer rooms.

Jesus promised exactly this kind of peace. The night before His crucifixion, knowing His disciples would soon walk into the most disordered season of their lives, He said to them, "Peace I leave with you; my peace I give you. I do not give to you as the world gives. Do not let your hearts be troubled and do not be afraid" (John 14:27). He differentiates His peace from the world's peace. The world's peace is circumstantial: it is absence of conflict, accumulation of security, achievement of comfort. When the circumstances shift, that peace disappears.

The peace Jesus gives does not depend on circumstances; it is the presence of the Spirit in the core, and the Spirit does not leave when the circumstances deteriorate. Paul describes the same phenomenon: "And the peace of God, which transcends all understanding, will guard your hearts and your minds in Christ Jesus" (Philippians 4:7). The peace "transcends understanding" because it does not correlate with visible conditions. It is an inner stability that outlasts outer instability.

> *"Peace I leave with you; my peace I give you. I do not give to you as the world gives. Do not let your hearts be troubled and do not be afraid."*
>
> **– John 14:27 (NIV)**

> *"Do not be anxious about anything, but in every situation, by prayer and petition, with thanksgiving, present your requests to God. And the peace of God, which transcends all understanding, will guard your hearts and your minds in Christ Jesus."*
>
> **– Philippians 4:6-7 (NIV)**

This does not mean the restored person is incapable of fear, sadness, or distress. Jesus Himself, in Gethsemane, was "sorrowful and troubled" (Matthew 26:37) and sweated as though with drops of blood. The restored life is not a life without emotion; it is a life in which emotion no longer has the final say. The anxious thought arises, but it is met by a deeper, settled confidence that the Source is still in control. The grief descends, but it descends upon a foundation that the grief cannot crack. Paul puts this with characteristic realism: "We are hard pressed on every side, but not crushed; perplexed, but not in despair; persecuted, but not abandoned; struck down, but not destroyed" (2 Corinthians 4:8-9). Hard pressed, perplexed, persecuted, struck down—the circumstances are not gentle. But the italicized words describe the inner refusal to collapse, because the center is held by Another.

> *"We are hard pressed on every side, but not crushed; perplexed, but not in despair; persecuted, but not abandoned; struck down, but not destroyed."*
>
> **– 2 Corinthians 4:8-9 (NIV)**

A Reoriented Desire: Wanting What the Spirit Wants

The second mark of a restored system is a gradual reorientation of desire. Before regeneration, the human will pulls in a direction that is, at its root, pulling away from God. Even good behaviors are often performed by a will that fundamentally wants the self. After regeneration, the Spirit begins to retrain the want. Things that previously felt attractive begin to feel hollow; things that previously felt burdensome begin to feel desirable.

The person discovers, sometimes with surprise, that they now want to pray when they once found prayer dull, that they now hunger for the Scriptures when they once found them obscure, that they now feel drawn to holiness where they once felt drawn to compromise. This reorientation is not instantaneous, and it is uneven—certain desires shift quickly, others resist for years—but the overall direction of the want is changing.

Ezekiel prophesied this interior reorientation centuries before Christ. "I will give you a new heart and put a new spirit in you; I will remove from you your heart of stone and give you a heart of flesh. And I will put my Spirit in you and move you to follow my decrees and be careful to keep my laws" (Ezekiel 36:26-27). The key clause is "move you to follow." The Spirit does not only inform the restored person about God's decrees;

He moves the restored person to want to follow them. The heart of stone was a heart that could be told the good but could not be moved to do it. The heart of flesh is a heart that has recovered the capacity to be moved—by God, by truth, by love, by the Spirit's own whisper. The restored system has a soft center again, pliable to its Maker.

> *"I will give you a new heart and put a new spirit in you; I will remove from you your heart of stone and give you a heart of flesh. And I will put my Spirit in you and move you to follow my decrees and be careful to keep my laws."*

– Ezekiel 36:26-27 (NIV)

David writes of this reoriented desire in Psalm 37: "Take delight in the Lord, and he will give you the desires of your heart" (Psalm 37:4). The verse is often quoted as a promise that God will grant whatever the heart currently wants. That is not what the Hebrew actually says. The pattern is more radical: the delight in the Lord is itself the instrument by which the desires of the heart are reshaped, so that what the heart now desires is what the Lord is pleased to give. It is a promise not of wish-fulfillment but of want-reconstruction. The restored system, spending time in the presence of the Lord, finds its appetites being reorganized around what the Lord delights in. The food the soul craves changes. The pleasure the soul seeks changes. The direction the soul runs changes.

> *"Take delight in the Lord, and he will give you the desires of your heart."*
>
> – Psalm 37:4 (NIV)

The practical texture of this reorientation can be surprising to new believers, who sometimes expect the old desires to vanish cleanly on the day of conversion. In reality, the old wants often persist, sometimes fiercely, while the new wants grow beside them. Paul describes his own experience of this dual pull: "For I do not do the good I want to do, but the evil I do not want to do—this I keep on doing" (Romans 7:19).

The struggle is not evidence that restoration has failed; it is evidence that restoration has begun. Before restoration, there was only one want: the flesh. Now there are two wants: the flesh still speaks, but a new and stronger voice from the indwelling Spirit contradicts it. The maturing believer learns to align with the Spirit's want over time, not by white-knuckled willpower, but by the steady practice of yielding, repenting, receiving, and walking forward.

A Renewed Mind: Thinking in the Shape of Truth

The third mark of a restored system is a renewed mind. Paul writes to the Romans: "Do not conform to the pattern of this world, but be transformed by the renewing of your mind. Then you will be able to test and approve what God's will is—his good, pleasing and perfect will" (Romans 12:2). The renewal of the mind is not a single event but a continuous retraining of the cognitive faculty away from the patterns of a corrupted world and toward the patterns of the kingdom. Where the world trains the mind to ask first, "What is best for me?" the Spirit retrains the mind to ask first, "What glorifies God and loves my neighbor?" Where the world trains the mind to assess reality by what is visible, the Spirit retrains the mind to assess reality by what is true according to the Word. Where the world trains the mind to protect the ego, the Spirit retrains the mind to protect the truth even when the truth costs the ego.

> *"Do not conform to the pattern of this world, but be transformed by the renewing of your mind. Then you will be able to test and approve what God's will is—his good, pleasing and perfect will."*
>
> **– Romans 12:2 (NIV)**

Practically, this renewal happens through sustained exposure to Scripture, prayerful reflection, and the company of other renewed minds. Paul tells the Philippians: "Whatever is true, whatever is noble, whatever is right, whatever is pure, whatever is lovely, whatever is admirable—if anything is excellent or praiseworthy—think about such things" (Philippians 4:8). The cognitive diet of the restored person is intentional. Just as the body becomes what it eats, the mind becomes what it considers. If the inputs are continuous cynicism, outrage, and triviality, the mind will take on those shapes. If the inputs are truth, nobility, rightness, and beauty, the mind will slowly be shaped into those contours. The renewed mind is not produced by accident; it is produced by the steady cultivation of what it is fed.

> *"Finally, brothers and sisters, whatever is true, whatever is noble, whatever is right, whatever is pure, whatever is lovely, whatever is admirable—if anything is excellent or praiseworthy—think about such things."*
>
> **– Philippians 4:8 (NIV)**

The renewed mind is also a mind that takes captive its own thoughts. Paul writes: "We demolish arguments and every pretension that sets itself up against the knowledge of God, and we take captive every thought to make it obedient to Christ" (2

Corinthians 10:5). The image is military. The mind is a battlefield, and every thought that crosses it is interrogated. The restored person does not accept every internal thought as self; he recognizes that thoughts arise from many sources—the flesh, the world, the Spirit, the enemy, plain fatigue—and learns to examine thoughts before acting on them. The anxious thought is questioned: "Is this true?" The resentful thought is questioned: "Does this match how Christ loved me when I did not deserve it?" The despairing thought is questioned: "What does God say about my future, not merely what do I feel about it?" The renewed mind is not a passive receptacle for every impulse; it is an active filter, trained by the Spirit to recognize the shape of truth.

> *"We demolish arguments and every pretension that sets itself up against the knowledge of God, and we take captive every thought to make it obedient to Christ."*
>
> **– 2 Corinthians 10:5 (NIV)**

A Redirected Body: Members as Instruments of Righteousness

The fourth mark of a restored system is a redirected body. The hardware that was once used to execute corrupted commands is reassigned to a new purpose. Paul writes, "Do not offer any part of yourself to sin as an instrument of wickedness, but rather offer yourselves to God as those who have been brought from death to life; and offer every part of yourself to him as an instrument of righteousness" (Romans 6:13). The body is not the enemy of the soul; it is the instrument through which the soul's new allegiance is physically expressed. The eyes that once consumed what corrupted the soul now read what feeds it. The ears that once listened to the mocking of the world now listen to the preaching of the Word. The mouth that once lied and cursed now tells the truth and blesses. The hands that once took now give. The feet that once ran toward sin now walk toward the needy. The body, restored in its purpose, becomes a theater in which the Spirit's new life is publicly performed.

> *"Do not offer any part of yourself to sin as an instrument of wickedness, but rather offer yourselves to God as those who have been brought from death to life; and offer every part of yourself to him as an instrument of righteousness."*
>
> **– Romans 6:13 (NIV)**

Paul elsewhere intensifies this redirection by describing the body as a temple. "Do you not know that your bodies are temples of the Holy Spirit, who is in you, whom you have received from God? You are not your own; you were bought at a price. Therefore honor God with your bodies" (1 Corinthians 6:19-20). This passage would have stunned first-century readers. Temples were the most sacred architecture of the ancient world; they were where gods were said to dwell.

To say that the ordinary body of an ordinary believer was now the dwelling place of the Spirit of the living God was to redefine the sacred. Restoration reorients the body's status. The body is no longer merely a personal possession to be used for personal pleasure; it is the temple of the Living God, and how it is treated—what is eaten, what is drunk, what is indulged, what is exhausted, what is given in sexual intimacy, what is withheld—matters theologically, not merely biologically.

> *"Do you not know that your bodies are temples of the Holy Spirit, who is in you, whom you have received from God? You are not your own; you were bought at a price. Therefore honor God with your bodies."*
>
> **– 1 Corinthians 6:19-20 (NIV)**

This does not mean the body is worshiped, nor that it is treated as a project. Christian history contains many distortions in which the body was either idolized or abused, and both distortions miss the balance of Scripture. The redirected body is honored as a temple, stewarded with moderation, disciplined with grace, and deployed as an instrument of the Spirit. It is not denied its legitimate needs; it is not enslaved to its illegitimate wants. It is ruled, in the biblical sense of ruled—governed by a restored spirit in submission to the Spirit of God.

Alignment and the Interface: When the Code Reaches the Hardware

There is a further, delicate dimension of the restored life that must be handled with care. The human being is not a disembodied spirit; the human being is a spirit interfaced with a body. That interface is where code becomes visible. When the spirit is aligned with the

Source, something begins to be transmitted through the interface that was not transmitted before. This is not a mechanical claim, and it must not be overclaimed. But Scripture teaches, and history bears witness, that spiritual alignment does, in fact, affect the interface through which we meet the world. The question is how, and under what limits.

The most obvious witness to this reality is Jesus Himself. In Him, the spirit was in perfect, unbroken alignment with the Source, and the effect on His interface was undeniable. He touched a leper, and the leprosy left (Mark 1:41-42). He spoke to a storm, and the storm went silent (Mark 4:39). He called dead children by name, and they opened their eyes (Mark 5:41-42). These were not magic tricks. They were the visible output of a human being through whom uncorrupted code was running without obstruction. The interface between spirit and world, in Jesus, was operating exactly as humanity was originally designed to operate—under the authority of a spirit in perfect communion with the Father. He said so explicitly: "The Son can do nothing by himself; he can do only what he sees his Father doing" (John 5:19). Alignment was the source of His authority. The interface was the channel of its expression.

> *"Jesus was indignant. He reached out his hand and touched the man. 'I am willing,' he said. 'Be clean!' Immediately the leprosy left him and he was cleansed."*
>
> **– Mark 1:41-42 (NIV)**

> *"Very truly I tell you, the Son can do nothing by himself; he can do only what he sees his Father doing, because whatever the Father does the Son also does."*
>
> **– John 5:19 (NIV)**

Jesus then extended this pattern to His followers, but again with the source of the authority carefully specified. He sent the Twelve, and later the Seventy-two, with authority to heal and to cast out demons. When they returned rejoicing that even the demons submitted to them, He redirected their joy to the deeper ground: "However, do not rejoice that the spirits submit to you, but rejoice that your names are written in heaven" (Luke 10:20). The authority was real, but it was not theirs. It flowed from their being joined to Him. Interface effects in the disciples were derivative of alignment with Jesus, just as Jesus's interface effects were derivative of alignment with the Father. The chain of authority was not severed; it was extended.

> *"The seventy-two returned with joy and said, 'Lord, even the demons submit to us in your name.'... 'I have given you authority to trample on snakes and scorpions and to overcome all the power of the enemy; nothing will harm you. However, do not rejoice that the spirits submit to you, but rejoice that your names are written in heaven.'"*
>
> **– Luke 10:17,19-20 (NIV)**

Alignment Affects the Interface—But Not as a Transaction

This has to be said carefully, because every generation of the church has included teachers who overclaim, promising that if you only have enough faith, or enough alignment, healing is guaranteed, prosperity is assured, and the interface will always behave. This is not what Scripture teaches. Paul himself, a man of extraordinary alignment, asked three times for a thorn in his flesh to be removed and was told no. "My grace is sufficient for you, for my power is made perfect in weakness" (2 Corinthians 12:9).

Timothy had chronic stomach problems; Paul counseled him to use a little wine for his frequent illnesses (1 Timothy 5:23). Trophimus was left sick at Miletus (2 Timothy 4:20). Epaphroditus nearly died of illness (Philippians 2:27). Lazarus, the dear friend of Jesus, died before Jesus arrived—and was raised, not because his alignment was sufficient, but because Jesus chose to do it (John 11). The record of Scripture refuses the tidy formula that would say, "Align yourself correctly and your body will always cooperate." The interface is affected by alignment; the interface is not controlled by alignment. God remains sovereign over what He does, when He does it, and for what purpose.

> *"But he said to me, 'My grace is sufficient for you, for my power is made perfect in weakness.' Therefore I will boast all the more gladly about my weaknesses, so that Christ's power may rest on me."*
>
> **– 2 Corinthians 12:9 (NIV)**

And yet. Scripture also refuses to say that alignment does nothing to the interface. James writes plainly: "Is anyone among you sick? Let them call the elders of the church to pray over them and anoint them with oil in the name of the Lord. And the prayer offered in faith will make the sick person well;

the Lord will raise them up. If they have sinned, they will be forgiven" (James 5:14-15). Healing is in the economy of the restored life. The church is not forbidden to pray for it; the church is commanded to pray for it. The condition of the spirit really does affect the condition of the body, not always and not predictably, but really. Paul, warning the Corinthians about partaking of the Lord's

Supper while holding unconfessed sin, writes, "That is why many among you are weak and sick, and a number of you have fallen asleep" (1 Corinthians 11:30). The spiritual and the physical are not sealed off from each other. They are interfaced. The spirit influences the body, and the body feeds back to the spirit. The restored person, aligned with the Source, often experiences tangible effects in the interface—better sleep, healed relationships, restored capacities, physical healings, unexpected protections, released addictions—not always, not on demand, and not in a way that vindicates any formula, but often enough that the Bible records it as part of the ordinary, expected landscape of the restored life.

> *"Is anyone among you sick? Let them call the elders of the church to pray over them and anoint them with oil in the name of the Lord. And the prayer offered in faith will make the sick person well; the Lord will raise them up. If they have sinned, they will be forgiven. Therefore confess your sins to each other and pray for each other so that you may be healed. The prayer of a righteous person is powerful and effective."*
>
> **– James 5:14-16 (NIV)**

How to Hold This Honestly

The pastoral posture toward interface effects must therefore hold two truths together at the same time. One: the Source can and does touch the body through a spirit that is yielded to Him. The Scriptures are full of it; the history of the church is full of it; many believers have seen it in their own lives. Two: the Source remains sovereign. He is not leveraged by technique, and He is not obligated to any formula. The same Paul who raised Eutychus from the dead (Acts 20:9-10) was not healed of his thorn. The same Peter who raised Tabitha at Joppa (Acts 9:40-41) was eventually crucified in Rome. The interface is sometimes touched, and sometimes left in weakness so that His power may be made perfect in weakness. Both outcomes can be profoundly faithful. Both outcomes remain in His hands.

What the restored believer can say confidently is this: alignment with the Source does affect the whole system, body included, because you are one whole person, not a ghost wearing a body. Repentance lightens the weight on the chest. Forgiveness unclenches the jaw. Surrender slows the racing mind. Prayer calms the nervous system. Communion with God, over time, restores capacities that corruption had eroded. And in moments God chooses, the effect on the interface is dramatic—the cane put down, the addiction released, the tumor gone, the marriage restored. In moments He does not choose, the effect is quieter but still real—peace in the pain, strength to continue, patience to endure, love that outlasts the body's weakening. The restored life is not a magic show; it is a living communion, and the body participates in that communion, sometimes loudly, sometimes faithfully in the background. The interface is never separate from the code, and the code is never separate from the Author.

Reordered Relationships: Love That Mirrors the Source

The fifth mark of a restored system is the reordering of relationships. If the fundamental break in Genesis was relational—humanity alienated from God, and consequently from one another—then the fundamental mark of restoration will be relational as well. The restored person relates differently. The two great commandments that Jesus identified—love the Lord your God with all your heart, soul, mind, and strength, and love your neighbor as yourself (Mark 12:30-31)—become the operating principles of the restored life, not as imposed rules but as emerging capacities. The restored system can, at last, begin to do what it was designed to do: love.

> *"Love the Lord your God with all your heart and with all your soul and with all your mind and with all your strength. The second is this: Love your neighbor as yourself. There is no commandment greater than these."*
>
> **– Mark 12:30-31 (NIV)**

John makes this relational test of restoration unmistakable. "We know that we have passed from death to life, because we love each other. Anyone who does not love remains in death" (1 John 3:14). Love, in this passage, is not sentimental feeling; it is the observable, costly willingness to give the self for the good of another. The restored system develops this capacity. Not all at once—many believers begin their new life with significant relational wounds and unhealed patterns—but over time, the Spirit produces in them a love that begins to resemble the love they have received. They forgive more quickly. They bear more patiently. They speak more truthfully. They give more generously. They confess more readily. They are more slow to take offense and more quick to repair a breach. These are not superhuman feats; they are the natural output of a system that has been reconnected to its Source, and the Source is love.

> *"We know that we have passed from death to life, because we love each other. Anyone who does not love remains in death."*
>
> **– 1 John 3:14 (NIV)**

Paul's letter to the Ephesians expresses this relational restoration with particular clarity. Husbands are to love their wives as Christ loved the church (Ephesians 5:25). Wives are to respect their husbands (5:33). Parents are not to exasperate their children (6:4). Children are to honor their parents (6:1-3). Employees and employers are to serve one another as serving the Lord (6:5-9). Each relational instruction in Ephesians is rooted not in social convention but in the union of the believer with Christ. The restored system does not perform relationships by protocol; it performs them by participation in the self-giving love of the Source. Where this love is missing, the professed restoration is suspect; where it is present, it is the strongest public evidence that something has actually happened inside the person.

A Reclaimed Vocation: Work as Worship

The sixth mark of a restored system is a reclaimed vocation. The corrupted code turned work into toil—something performed for survival, status, or fear, with the dignity of creative partnership with God largely lost. The restored system begins to recover the original vocation of humanity: to reflect the image of God into the world through the work of the hands. Paul writes to the Colossians, "Whatever you do, work at it with all your heart, as working for the Lord, not for human masters" (Colossians 3:23). The sentence abolishes the sacred-secular divide. There is no secular work in the restored life; there is only work done unto the Lord or work done unto lesser gods. The accountant, the mother, the welder, the nurse, the student, the farmer, the artist—each has a vocation that, when performed as unto the Lord, becomes a form of worship. The hands that tighten the bolt, the voice that explains the concept, the body that lifts the child, the mind that debugs the code—each is offered back to the Source who gave them.

> *"Whatever you do, work at it with all your heart, as working for the Lord, not for human masters, since you know that you will receive an inheritance from the Lord as a reward. It is the Lord Christ you are serving."*
>
> **– Colossians 3:23-24 (NIV)**

This reclaiming of vocation changes the felt texture of ordinary labor. Work done as worship is not freed from difficulty, but it is freed from futility. The Preacher of Ecclesiastes, surveying work from the vantage point of a life apart from God, called it meaningless; Paul, surveying work from the vantage point of a life restored to God, called it inheritance. The same activity, done under two different headships, produces two different internal experiences. The restored person is not working to build a kingdom for himself; he is participating in the building of a kingdom whose architect is God. This makes both the excellence and the rest of work possible. Excellence, because the work is for the Lord and therefore deserves real quality. Rest, because the outcome is in His hands and not ultimately in the worker's.

An Expanded Horizon: Eternity Reframes the Present

The seventh mark of a restored system is an expanded horizon. The corrupted code shrinks the human horizon to the span of one mortal life, and within that span to the immediate moment. The restored code expands the horizon to eternity. Paul writes, "Therefore we do not lose heart. Though outwardly we are wasting away, yet inwardly we are being renewed day by day. For our light and momentary troubles are achieving for us an eternal glory that far outweighs them all. So we fix our eyes not on what is seen, but on what is unseen, since what is seen is temporary, but what is unseen is eternal" (2 Corinthians 4:16-18). The passage does not deny present suffering; it reframes it. The troubles are called "light and momentary" not because Paul thought they were small in the feeling, but because he had developed a scale against which they were small in the reckoning. That scale is eternity.

> *"Therefore we do not lose heart. Though outwardly we are wasting away, yet inwardly we are being renewed day by day. For our light and momentary troubles are achieving for us an eternal glory that far outweighs them all. So we fix our eyes not on what is seen, but on what is unseen, since what is seen is temporary, but what is unseen is eternal."*

– 2 Corinthians 4:16-18 (NIV)

This expanded horizon gives the restored person a different kind of patience, a different kind of courage, and a different kind of freedom. Patience, because the final accounting is not owed by the end of the week; it is owed in the age to come. Courage, because death has lost its final authority over the one for whom life is "Christ to live and gain to die" (Philippians 1:21). Freedom, because nothing of eternal significance can be taken away by temporal loss.

The restored person does not become indifferent to the present—quite the opposite; the present becomes freighted with eternal meaning. But the present no longer carries the whole weight of his hope. His hope is anchored in a place that no storm in the present can reach. "We have this hope as an anchor for the soul, firm and secure. It enters the inner sanctuary behind the curtain" (Hebrews 6:19).

> *"We have this hope as an anchor for the soul, firm and secure. It enters the inner sanctuary behind the curtain."*

– Hebrews 6:19 (NIV)

A Restored Voice: Speech in the Shape of the Source

The eighth mark of a restored system is a restored voice. Words were among the first gifts God gave to humanity in the garden, where Adam named the animals (Genesis 2:19-20), and words are among the earliest casualties of the fall, where Adam and Eve use speech to hide, blame, and evade (Genesis 3:10-13). James devotes an entire chapter to the power of the tongue, calling it "a fire, a world of evil among the parts of the body. It corrupts the whole person" (James 3:6), and then observing with pained honesty that "with the tongue we praise our Lord and Father, and with it we curse human beings, who have been made in God's likeness.

Out of the same mouth come praise and cursing. My brothers and sisters, this should not be" (James 3:9-10). The restored voice is not the voice that can never misspeak; it is the voice that is progressively being brought into alignment with the Source. Its cursing diminishes. Its blessing grows. Its truth-telling strengthens. Its gossip withers. Its complaint softens. Its praise swells.

> *"With the tongue we praise our Lord and Father, and with it we curse human beings, who have been made in God's likeness. Out of the same mouth come praise and cursing. My brothers and sisters, this should not be."*
>
> **– James 3:9-10 (NIV)**

Paul instructs the Ephesians: "Do not let any unwholesome talk come out of your mouths, but only what is helpful for building others up according to their needs, that it may benefit those who listen" (Ephesians 4:29). The standard is specific: speech is to be evaluated by whether it builds up the hearer. The restored person is not perfectly consistent in this, but he or she is being retrained. The old habit of speaking to release frustration at another's expense is being exchanged for the new habit of speaking to edify. The old habit of exaggerating is being exchanged for the new habit of honoring truth. The old habit of cynicism is being exchanged for the new habit of hope. Over years, the shape of the tongue changes, because the heart behind the tongue is being changed, and out of the heart the mouth speaks (Matthew 12:34).

> *"Do not let any unwholesome talk come out of your mouths, but only what is helpful for building others up according to their needs, that it may benefit those who listen."*
>
> **– Ephesians 4:29 (NIV)**

A Stable Center Amid an Unstable World

The cumulative effect of these marks is a human being who possesses, perhaps for the first time, a stable center amid an unstable world. The world does not become less unstable; anything, in the closing age, it becomes more unstable. But the restored person is anchored in a center that the instability cannot dislodge. The writer of Hebrews describes believers as those who have "fled to take hold of the hope set before us. We have this hope as an anchor for the soul, firm and secure" (Hebrews 6:18-19).

Peter similarly writes to believers suffering persecution: "In all this you greatly rejoice, though now for a little while you may have had to suffer grief in all kinds of trials. These have come so that the proven genuineness of your faith... may result in praise, glory and honor when Jesus Christ is revealed" (1 Peter 1:6-7). The trials are not avoided; they are passed through with a center that holds.

> *"In all this you greatly rejoice, though now for a little while you may have had to suffer grief in all kinds of trials. These have come so that the proven genuineness of your faith—of greater worth than gold, which perishes even though refined by fire—may result in praise, glory and honor when Jesus Christ is revealed."*
>
> **– 1 Peter 1:6-7 (NIV)**

The watching world is often the first to notice this stability. The neighbor who suffers without bitterness, the coworker who forgives without performance, the parent who endures sleepless seasons without collapse, the widow who grieves without despair—these are visible signatures of a system running on code the world does not have. Peter counsels believers to be ready: "Always be prepared to give an answer to everyone who asks you to give the reason for the hope that you have. But do this with gentleness and respect" (1 Peter 3:15).

The question is posed not because the believer has preached at the neighbor, but because the neighbor has seen something and wants to know where it came from. The restored life is, in this sense, quietly evangelistic. It does not need to argue its case at every moment; it lives its case, and the case often speaks more loudly than the words.

A Community of Restored Systems

Finally, the restored life is not a solitary life. The individual has been regenerated, but the individual has been regenerated into a body—the body of Christ, the church. Paul uses the metaphor of the body relentlessly, because it captures the interdependence that restoration creates. "For just as each of us has one body with many members, and these members do not all have the same function, so in Christ we, though many, form one body, and each member belongs to all the others" (Romans 12:4-5). The restored system is not an individual server running its own software; it is a node in a larger network, designed to communicate with, receive from, and contribute to other restored systems. A restored person in isolation is vulnerable, because sanctification happens most reliably in the friction and comfort of community. A restored person in community is strengthened, because the gifts of the Spirit are distributed across many, and each member supplies what the others lack.

> *"For just as each of us has one body with many members, and these members do not all have the same function, so in Christ we, though many, form one body, and each member belongs to all the others."*
>
> **– Romans 12:4-5 (NIV)**

The letter to the Hebrews calls this community indispensable: "And let us consider how we may spur one another on toward love and good deeds, not giving up meeting together, as some are in the habit of doing, but encouraging one another—and all the more as you see the Day approaching" (Hebrews 10:24-25). The passage is often cited as a mandate to attend services, but its deeper point is that restored systems need one another. The spur that moves one toward love and good deeds often comes through the voice of another believer.

The encouragement that sustains one through suffering often comes through the presence of another believer. The restored life is lived, biblically, in a restored community. Those who try to live the restored life apart from the body of Christ usually find their fire cooling, their doctrine drifting, and their character eroding, not because they were insincere, but because the Spirit's ordinary means of sustaining restoration include the brothers and sisters He has placed around them.

> *"And let us consider how we may spur one another on toward love and good deeds, not giving up meeting together, as some are in the habit of doing, but encouraging one another—and all the more as you see the Day approaching."*
>
> **– Hebrews 10:24-25 (NIV)**

To live restored, then, is to live as love—at peace, with reoriented desires, a renewed mind, a redirected body, an interface that shows the effects of alignment, reordered relationships, a reclaimed vocation, an expanded horizon, a healing voice, a stable center, and an active place in the body of Christ. These marks are not achieved all at once, and they are not achieved in any believer without imperfection. But they are the trajectory of the restored life, the direction in which the Holy Spirit is carrying the regenerated system, and the taste of the life that was originally designed. The final chapter turns to the culmination of that design: the restoration of everything, when the Source who began the rewrite in the individual completes the rewrite in the whole creation.

CHAPTER 15

/ THE KINGDOM

The Kingdom

The Final Restoration of All Systems

Every story in Scripture bends toward a single horizon. From the first chapters of Genesis to the final chapters of Revelation, the Bible is moving—often through shadows and across long centuries—toward the restoration of all things. The Source who breathed life into the first human being in a garden has not abandoned His project. He has, in Christ, begun the process of rewriting the corrupted code in individual believers, and He has already secured, in the cross and resurrection, the final restoration of the creation as a whole.

The personal restoration traced in the previous chapters is not the end of the story; it is a deposit, a foretaste, a first installment of a restoration whose full shape is unveiled only at the end. The kingdom of God is the name Scripture gives to this final, cosmic operating state, in which every system—personal, relational, communal, ecological, and political—runs once again on the Source Code it was originally designed to run on.

Jesus's central message was the kingdom. Mark summarizes His opening ministry with the line, "The time has come," he said. "The kingdom of God has come near. Repent and believe the good news!" (Mark 1:15). He taught His disciples to pray for it: "Your kingdom come, your will be done, on earth as it is in heaven" (Matthew 6:10). He told parable after parable about it, comparing it to a mustard seed that grows into a tree, to yeast that leavens the whole lump, to a treasure buried in a field, to a pearl of great price, to a net full of fish, to a king who returns from a journey. The kingdom, in Jesus's preaching, is not merely a future place; it is the active reign of God breaking into the present and advancing toward a final consummation.

The kingdom began in His ministry, spreads through His church, and culminates at His return.

> *"The time has come. The kingdom of God has come near. Repent and believe the good news!"*
>
> **– Mark 1:15 (NIV)**

> *"Your kingdom come, your will be done, on earth as it is in heaven."*
>
> **– Matthew 6:10 (NIV)**

Already and Not Yet: The Kingdom in Two Tenses

The New Testament speaks of the kingdom in two tenses, and both tenses must be held together if the biblical picture is to stay in focus. On one hand, the kingdom has already come. Jesus said to the Pharisees, "The kingdom of God is in your midst" (Luke 17:21), meaning that His own presence as the promised King had inaugurated the reign. He cast out demons by the Spirit of God, and so the kingdom of God had come upon them (Matthew 12:28). Through the cross, the resurrection, and the pouring out of the Spirit at Pentecost, the kingdom has broken decisively into the world. On the other hand, the kingdom has not yet arrived in its full form. Jesus still taught His disciples to pray for its coming. Paul wrote of a future day when Christ would hand over the kingdom to God the Father, having destroyed every dominion and power, and when "the last enemy to be destroyed is death" (1 Corinthians 15:26). The kingdom is already—and not yet. It is present, and it is coming.

> *"For he must reign until he has put all his enemies under his feet. The last enemy to be destroyed is death."*
>
> **– 1 Corinthians 15:25-26 (NIV)**

This two-tense reality shapes how restored believers live. They do not despair that the world is still broken, because they know the kingdom has begun. They do not pretend that the world is already fixed, because they know the kingdom has not yet fully arrived. They live, in the words of the apostle, as "citizens of heaven" (Philippians 3:20) still residing in the present age, participating in both the first fruits of the kingdom now and the full harvest that is coming. This posture allows them to work for justice, mercy, and renewal in the present without being crushed when those efforts meet resistance or fall short. The final restoration does not depend on them; it depends on the One whose return will complete what His cross secured.

The Defeat of the Virus: Sin, Death, and the Serpent Undone

Because the Bible has diagnosed the human condition as an infection—a virus that corrupted the code—its description of final restoration includes the decisive, permanent defeat of the virus itself. Sin is not tolerated, managed, or contained in the kingdom; it is purged. Death is not merely postponed; it is abolished. The serpent is not simply silenced; he is judged. Paul writes of this in language that echoes Genesis 3:15, the first gospel promise: "The God of peace will soon crush Satan under your feet" (Romans 16:20).

The crushing does not wound the restored system in passing; it is the final execution of the judgment announced at the fall. Revelation describes it graphically: "And the devil, who deceived them, was thrown into the lake of burning sulfur, where the beast and the false prophet had been thrown. They will be tormented day and night for ever and ever" (Revelation 20:10). Whatever one's interpretation of the imagery, the point is unmistakable. The source of the infection is ended. The accuser is silenced permanently.

> *"The God of peace will soon crush Satan under your feet. The grace of our Lord Jesus be with you."*

– Romans 16:20 (NIV)

Death, too, is undone. Paul writes with almost audible triumph, "When the perishable has been clothed with the imperishable, and the mortal with immortality, then the saying that is written will come true: 'Death has been swallowed up in victory.' 'Where, O death, is your victory? Where, O death, is your sting?' The sting of death is sin, and the power of sin is the law. But thanks be to God! He gives us the victory through our Lord Jesus Christ" (1 Corinthians 15:54-57). Death, the last visible enforcement of the fall, is abolished. The grave, which has been filling with bodies for every generation since Adam, will be emptied. The cemeteries will yield up what they hold. The ancient corruption will be reversed not only spiritually, which is the present experience of believers, but also bodily, visibly, and publicly, in the resurrection of the dead.

> *"When the perishable has been clothed with the imperishable, and the mortal with immortality, then the saying that is written will come true: 'Death has been swallowed up in victory.' 'Where, O death, is your victory? Where, O death, is your sting?' The sting of death is sin, and the power of sin is the law. But thanks be to God! He gives us the victory through our Lord Jesus Christ."*

– 1 Corinthians 15:54-57 (NIV)

Resurrection: The Hardware Restored

A central Christian claim, often neglected in popular preaching, is that salvation is not merely a soul-rescue but a whole-person restoration that includes the body. The biblical hope is not escape from the body but the transformation of the body. Paul writes that the Lord Jesus Christ "by the power that enables him to bring everything under his control, will transform our lowly bodies so that they will be like his glorious body" (Philippians 3:21). The body is not abandoned in the restoration; it is upgraded. The hardware that has groaned under the virus, that has wept and bled and aged and failed, is restored to a form that matches the risen body of Christ—still recognizable, still physical, still embodied, but no longer subject to decay.

> *"But our citizenship is in heaven. And we eagerly await a Savior from there, the Lord Jesus Christ, who, by the power that enables him to bring everything under his control, will transform our lowly bodies so that they will be like his glorious body."*
>
> **– Philippians 3:20-21 (NIV)**

Paul's resurrection chapter, 1 Corinthians 15, gives the most extended description of this transformation. He uses the metaphor of a seed and a plant to convey both continuity and transformation: "What you sow does not come to life unless it dies. When you sow, you do not plant the body that will be, but just a seed... So will it be with the resurrection of the dead.

The body that is sown is perishable, it is raised imperishable; it is sown in dishonor, it is raised in glory; it is sown in weakness, it is raised in power; it is sown a natural body, it is raised a spiritual body" (1 Corinthians 15:36-44). The resurrection body is the same body in the sense that the plant is the same as the seed—continuous, organic, connected—but different in the sense that it operates in a different mode. It is imperishable, glorious, powerful, spiritual. The hardware has been re-engineered. The hardware has finally come home to its design.

> *"So will it be with the resurrection of the dead. The body that is sown is perishable, it is raised imperishable; it is sown in dishonor, it is raised in glory; it is sown in weakness, it is raised in power; it is sown a natural body, it is raised a spiritual body."*
>
> **– 1 Corinthians 15:42-44 (NIV)**

A New Heaven and a New Earth: The Creation Restored

The restoration extends beyond the individual body to the entire creation. The same Scriptures that describe the fall as affecting the ground (Genesis 3:17-18) and bringing death into the biosphere describe the restoration as including the whole creation. Paul writes: "For the creation waits in eager expectation for the children of God to be revealed. For the creation was subjected to frustration, not by its own choice, but by the will of the one who subjected it, in hope that the creation itself will be liberated from its bondage to decay and brought into the freedom and glory of the children of God.

We know that the whole creation has been groaning as in the pains of childbirth right up to the present time" (Romans 8:19-22). The language is astonishing. The physical creation is portrayed as a patient sufferer who has been waiting for a liberation that will come when the children of God are fully revealed. The rivers and forests and mountains and seas are not disposable scenery; they are participants in the story, and their restoration is part of the promised end.

> *"For the creation waits in eager expectation for the children of God to be revealed. For the creation was subjected to frustration, not by its own choice, but by the will of the one who subjected it, in hope that the creation itself will be liberated from its bondage to decay and brought into the freedom and glory of the children of God. We know that the whole creation has been groaning as in the pains of childbirth right up to the present time."*
>
> **– Romans 8:19-22 (NIV)**

John's Revelation gives us the grand vision. "Then I saw 'a new heaven and a new earth,' for the first heaven and the first earth had passed away, and there was no longer any sea. I saw the Holy City, the new Jerusalem, coming down out of heaven from God, prepared as a bride beautifully dressed for her husband. And I heard a loud voice from the throne saying, 'Look! God's dwelling place is now among the people, and he will dwell with them. They will be his people, and God himself will be with them and be their God. He will wipe every tear from their eyes. There will be no more death or mourning or crying or pain, for the old order of things has passed away'" (Revelation 21:1-4).

Every clause in this passage reverses something that the fall introduced. The separation between God and humanity is ended; He dwells with His people again. The tears are wiped; the sorrow that has watered every human generation is dried. Death is gone. Mourning is gone. Crying is gone. Pain is gone. The old order—the order under which the virus ran and everything it touched malfunctioned—has passed away.

> *"Then I saw 'a new heaven and a new earth,' for the first heaven and the first earth had passed away, and there was no longer any sea. I saw the Holy City, the new Jerusalem, coming down out of heaven from God, prepared as a bride beautifully dressed for her husband. And I heard a loud voice from the throne saying, 'Look! God's dwelling place is now among the people, and he will dwell with them. They will be his people, and God himself will be with them and be their God. He will wipe every tear from their eyes. There will be no more death or mourning or crying or pain, for the old order of things has passed away.'"*
>
> **– Revelation 21:1-4 (NIV)**

The next verse is perhaps the most theologically significant of all: "He who was seated on the throne said, 'I am making everything new!'" (Revelation 21:5). The verb is present continuous. He is making everything new. Not replacing, not discarding, not annihilating—making new. The Greek word kainos, translated new, connotes renewal, not replacement. The new creation is not an entirely different thing from the old; it is the old restored to what it was always meant to be. The heavens and the earth are not scrapped; they are redeemed. The body is not abandoned; it is resurrected. The human being is not canceled; the human being is brought, at last, to the operating state for which the Source originally wrote the code.

> *"He who was seated on the throne said, 'I am making everything new!' Then he said, 'Write this down, for these words are trustworthy and true.'"*
>
> **– Revelation 21:5 (NIV)**

The Return of the Source: God Dwelling with His People

The climactic feature of the restored creation is not any particular architecture or environmental feature. It is the presence of God with His people. "Look! God's dwelling place is now among the people" (Revelation 21:3). The fall in Genesis 3 ended with humanity expelled from Eden, cherubim posted at the entrance, and a flaming sword guarding the tree of life (Genesis 3:24). The entire arc of biblical history is the story of how God, without compromising His holiness, makes His way back to His creatures. The tabernacle is a portable hint of it. The temple is a more permanent hint of it. The incarnation is a personal, embodied fulfillment of it: "The Word became flesh and made his dwelling among us" (John 1:14). The Spirit's indwelling of the believer is an interior, individual installment of it. And the new Jerusalem is the cosmic, everlasting, final realization of it. God dwells with His people, fully, visibly, permanently.

> *"And I heard a loud voice from the throne saying, 'Look! God's dwelling place is now among the people, and he will dwell with them. They will be his people, and God himself will be with them and be their God.'"*
>
> **– Revelation 21:3 (NIV)**

John notes a striking detail about the new Jerusalem: "I did not see a temple in the city, because the Lord God Almighty and the Lamb are its temple" (Revelation 21:22). Every previous religious system in biblical history had a building where God was said to be more present than elsewhere. The new creation has no such building, not because God is less present, but because He is everywhere present. The whole city is a temple, because God Himself fills it. The dichotomy between sacred space and secular space that has marked every corrupted civilization is finally abolished. There is no portion of the new creation that is not saturated with His presence. The whole system, at last, runs on the Source at every point.

> *"I did not see a temple in the city, because the Lord God Almighty and the Lamb are its temple. The city does not need the sun or the moon to shine on it, for the glory of God gives it light, and the Lamb is its lamp."*
>
> **– Revelation 21:22-23 (NIV)**

The River, the Tree, and the Face: Eden Surpassed

The final chapter of the Bible deliberately echoes its first. In Genesis 2, there was a river that watered the garden and divided into four headwaters (Genesis 2:10-14). In Revelation 22, John writes: "Then the angel showed me the river of the water of life, as clear as crystal, flowing from the throne of God and of the Lamb down the middle of the great street of the city" (Revelation 22:1). In Genesis 2, there was a tree of life in the middle of the garden (Genesis 2:9), from which humanity was later cut off (Genesis 3:22-24). In Revelation 22, the tree of life returns: "On each side of the river stood the tree of life, bearing twelve crops of fruit, yielding its fruit every month. And the leaves of the tree are for the healing of the nations" (Revelation 22:2). The exile that began when humanity was banished from the presence of the tree ends when the tree is planted, abundantly, in the city of God, freely available, healing the nations.

> *"Then the angel showed me the river of the water of life, as clear as crystal, flowing from the throne of God and of the Lamb down the middle of the great street of the city. On each side of the river stood the tree of life, bearing twelve crops of fruit, yielding its fruit every month. And the leaves of the tree are for the healing of the nations."*

– Revelation 22:1-2 (NIV)

And there is one more echo, perhaps the most tender. Genesis ends with Adam and Eve hiding from the presence of the Lord among the trees (Genesis 3:8). Revelation ends with their descendants no longer hiding. "They will see his face, and his name will be on their foreheads" (Revelation 22:4). This is the reversal of the deepest damage of the fall. The alienation from the face of God is ended. What Moses could not behold and live (Exodus 33:20), what the patriarchs glimpsed only in visions, what the prophets spoke of from a distance, what the disciples saw in a veiled form in the transfigured Christ—this is now the ordinary experience of the restored community. They see His face. The hidden have been revealed. The distant have been brought near. The orphans have come home.

> *"No longer will there be any curse. The throne of God and of the Lamb will be in the city, and his servants will serve him. They will see his face, and his name will be on their foreheads."*

– Revelation 22:3-4 (NIV)

The Bible, remarkably, ends not in a garden but in a city. Eden was a garden; the new Jerusalem is a city. The creation has not merely been reset to its starting condition; it has been advanced to its mature condition. The potential that lay dormant in the garden has been developed into the culture of the city. The humanity that began as two stewards has grown into an unnumbered multitude from every tribe and language and people and nation (Revelation 7:9). The kingdom is not a return to naive innocence; it is the fruition of a creation that has journeyed through history and arrived, finally, at what it was always becoming. The Source Code, running at last without corruption, produces not regression but glorious completion.

The Invitation: Living Toward the Kingdom

The last chapter of Revelation, and therefore the last chapter of the Bible, closes with an invitation that is both personal and cosmic. "The Spirit and the bride say, 'Come!' And let the one who hears say, 'Come!' Let the one who is thirsty come; and let the one who wishes take the free gift of the water of life" (Revelation 22:17). The entire story of Scripture funnels into this sentence. The Spirit—who has been moving over the waters since Genesis, breathing into Adam, indwelling the prophets, and now filling the church—joins with the bride, the restored community of God's people, in a single word of invitation: Come. The One who would otherwise never be reached has made Himself reachable. The water that the broken cisterns could not hold is poured out as a free gift. The only requirement is thirst. The only response is to come.

> *"The Spirit and the bride say, 'Come!' And let the one who hears say, 'Come!' Let the one who is thirsty come; and let the one who wishes take the free gift of the water of life."*
>
> **– Revelation 22:17 (NIV)**

Living toward the kingdom, then, has a distinct shape in the life of the believer. It means living with hope that the final restoration is assured, even when the current restoration is partial. It means living with urgency, because the King is coming and much remains to be done before He arrives. It means living with generosity, because the hand that expects a final inheritance can open freely in the present. It means living with courage, because no form of earthly loss can ultimately cost what heaven has already secured. It means living with longing, with the ache of one who has tasted the first fruits and now waits for the full harvest. The apostle John ends the canon with exactly this longing: "He who testifies to these things says, 'Yes, I am coming soon.' Amen. Come, Lord Jesus" (Revelation 22:20).

> *"He who testifies to these things says, 'Yes, I am coming soon.' Amen. Come, Lord Jesus."*
>
> **– Revelation 22:20 (NIV)**

The book of Scripture began with God speaking the world into being. It ends with the Spirit and the bride speaking an invitation to all who will hear. In between, the long, painful, and glorious story of the Source Code has been told: the original build, the viral corruption, the false fixes, the redemption, the restoration, the new creation. The reader who has followed this story to its end is invited to do more than read. The book has not merely described a system; it has held up a mirror to the reader's own. The malfunction that runs beneath every human life is real. The virus that began in Eden is still active in every heart. The false fixes that humanity has spent millennia constructing still promise relief that never comes. And the Source who breathed the first breath of life still offers, in Jesus Christ and by the Holy Spirit, to breathe the breath of new life into anyone who will receive it. The kingdom has come; the kingdom is coming; and the restoration of all systems is held securely in the hands of the One who began the work and will, without fail, carry it to completion. The conclusion that follows will return to the beginning and draw the whole picture together in a final word.

Back to the Source

A Final Word

This book has made a single, sustained argument. The human being is a system. That system was designed and activated by God Himself when He breathed the breath of life into Adam. That breath was the original Source Code—the spiritual operating instruction set that enabled a creature of dust to know, love, worship, and walk with its Creator. Apart from that breath, the human being is not diminished; the human being is not alive. The breath is not a feature; the breath is the life. When the virus entered the system in the garden, it did not merely damage a subroutine; it corrupted the very code that tied the creature to the Source. From that corruption flowed every malfunction the world has since endured: estranged relationships, broken bodies, warring nations, confused identities, failing institutions, and the long, slow catastrophe of death. Nothing has escaped the virus. Every system—personal, social, ecological—runs today under its influence.

Against this universal malfunction, humanity has constructed its own patches. Self-help has offered the illusion that the corrupted can repair themselves. Success has offered the illusion that accumulation can fill what connection was meant to fill. Pleasure has offered the illusion that sensation can silence a spiritual ache. Identity construction has offered the illusion that the self can define itself without reference to the Source whose image it bears. Religion without transformation has offered the most tragic illusion of all—an external form of godliness while the internal code continues to run corrupted. Each of these patches has helped some people in surface ways for a time, and each of these patches has, in the end, failed to reach the place where the virus actually lives. No human fix can overwrite divine code. The spiritual problem requires a spiritual solution, and the spiritual solution has come from outside the system.

The solution, Scripture declares and this book has traced, is the restoration of the Source Code through the Lord Jesus Christ and the indwelling of the Holy Spirit. In Christ, the legal break has been repaired: the penalty of the virus has been paid, and the believer stands justified before a righteous God. In the regeneration worked by the Holy Spirit, the core has been installed: the old spirit has been made alive, and the new life of God has been planted in the place where the virus used to rule. In sanctification, the ongoing rewrite continues: day by day, the Spirit retrains desires, renews minds, redirects bodies, reorders relationships, reclaims vocations, and reshapes voices, until the believer progressively resembles the One into whose image he or she is being conformed. And in the final kingdom, the restoration will be completed in the resurrection of the body, the renewal of the creation, and the unveiled presence of God dwelling with His people forever. The Source who began the rewrite will finish it.

All of this is an invitation. The book has described a salvation, but descriptions do not save. The breath has been offered, but the breath must be received. The Spirit and the bride still say, with the final voice of the canon, "Come." The reader who has walked through these pages with interest but has not yet received the restoration is invited, now, to do the one thing the corrupted system cannot do for itself. Confess that the virus is real, and that its presence is personal. Trust that Jesus Christ, in His death and resurrection, is sufficient to address what has broken. Ask the Holy Spirit to do the internal work that no external effort can reproduce. The invitation is simple because the gospel is simple. The cost has already been paid by Another. The work has already been done by Another. The only step the receiving heart takes is the step of coming.

To the reader who has already received this salvation but feels uncertain whether the restoration is real in his or her own life, take comfort. The marks of restoration are a trajectory, not a snapshot. The peace, the reoriented desire, the renewed mind, the redirected body, the reordered relationships, the reclaimed vocation, the expanded horizon, the healing voice—these grow. They are uneven. They are frequently interrupted. They are resisted at every turn by the remnants of the flesh, the pressure of the world, and the accusations of the enemy. But they grow. The One who began a good work in you will carry it on to completion until the day of Christ Jesus (Philippians 1:6). The completion is not your achievement; it is His commitment. Rest in that, and keep walking.

And to the reader who finds himself in a difficult season, where the malfunction in the world or the malfunction within seems overwhelming, remember the framework this book has laid out. You are not merely a body with a problem. You are a spirit, clothed in a body, designed to run on the breath of God. The solution to what ails you will not be found in a better routine, a better diagnosis, a better relationship, or a better distraction. The solution will be found in a deeper reception of the Source who indwells you and in the long patience of letting Him finish what He has begun. When pain is loud and prayer is difficult, remember that the Spirit Himself intercedes for you with groanings too deep for words (Romans 8:26). You are not alone in the system. The Source is closer than your breath. He is, in fact, your breath.

The book began with an image of a malfunctioning system. It ends with the image of that same system restored by the One who wrote its code. The distance between malfunction and restoration is bridged not by the strength of the creature but by the initiative of the Creator. The breath that first filled Adam has been offered again, in Christ, to every descendant of Adam who will receive it. The virus is being purged in the believer; the virus will be abolished in the creation. The bride is being prepared; the King is returning. The story that began in a garden will end in a city, and the Source who breathed the first breath will breathe eternally over His restored people. To that end, this book has pointed. To that end, every restored life points. To that end, the whole of Scripture points. And to that end, by His grace, the reader is invited to live, and to run, and to rest.

There is, finally, only one sentence that summarizes what these chapters have tried to communicate. Whatever the reader remembers from these pages, let it be this: You were not designed to function without the Source—you were designed to run on it.

— You were not designed to function without the Source—you were designed to run on it. —

References

Scripture Index and Notes

This book is, first and finally, a conversation with Scripture. The argument of The Original Source Code stands or falls on the faithfulness of its reading of the Bible, and the reader is invited — encouraged, even urged — to open the Scriptures and see whether these things are so.

All Scripture quotations in this book are taken from the Holy Bible, New International Version® (NIV®). Copyright © 1973, 1978, 1984, 2011 by Biblica, Inc.™ Used by permission. All rights reserved worldwide. Where the text engages the original Hebrew (ruach, neshamah, nephesh, yatsar, yetzer) or Greek (pneuma, psyche, nous, charaktēr, agapē, makrothumia, zoe), the transliterations and meanings follow standard lexical resources in common use among biblical scholars: the Brown-Driver-Briggs Hebrew and English Lexicon (BDB), the Hebrew and Aramaic Lexicon of the Old Testament (HALOT), A Greek-English Lexicon of the New Testament and Other Early Christian Literature (BDAG), and Strong's Exhaustive Concordance.

The reference list that follows records, chapter by chapter, the Scripture passages quoted or directly discussed in the body of the book. It is not an exhaustive catalogue of every allusion and echo; the Bible's voice is woven through these pages at a deeper level than any footnote could track. It is, rather, a study companion — a way for the reader who wishes to go further to sit with the same passages that shaped the thinking of these chapters, and to weigh them in their own reading.

The reader is also pointed, at appropriate places in the text, to the author's earlier book, Success, The Total Package, which offers the complementary positive treatment of what integrated human life looks like when all of its dimensions — achievement, relationships, character, purpose, and spirit — are running together rather than at cross-purposes.

Introduction — The Breath Before the Build

Genesis 1:1 *(NIV)*
Genesis 2:7 *(NIV)*
Job 32:8 *(NIV)*
Job 33:4 *(NIV)*
Psalm 104:29-30 *(NIV)*

Chapter 1 — The Build: Humanity as a Designed System

Genesis 1:27 *(NIV)*
Genesis 1:28 *(NIV)*
Genesis 2:7 *(NIV)*
Psalm 139:13-14 *(NIV)*
Proverbs 4:23 *(NIV)*
1 Thessalonians 5:23 *(NIV)*

Chapter 2 — The Breath: The Moment Humanity Came Online

Genesis 1:31 *(NIV)*
Genesis 2:7 *(NIV)*
Ecclesiastes 12:7 *(NIV)*
Ephesians 2:1 *(NIV)*
James 1:8 *(NIV)*

Chapter 3 — The Breach: The Virus Enters the System

Genesis 2:16-17 *(NIV)*
Genesis 3:1 *(NIV)*
Genesis 3:4-5 *(NIV)*
Genesis 3:7 *(NIV)*
Genesis 3:8 *(NIV)*
Genesis 3:12-13 *(NIV)*
Genesis 9:6 *(NIV)*
Jeremiah 2:13 *(NIV)*
2 Corinthians 11:3 *(NIV)*

Chapter 4 — Inherited Code: Transmission, Procreation, and Interface

Genesis 2:7 *(NIV)*
Job 14:4 *(NIV)*
Psalm 51:5 *(NIV)*
Jeremiah 17:9 *(NIV)*
Romans 3:10-12 *(NIV)*
Romans 5:12 *(NIV)*
Romans 5:19 *(NIV)*
Romans 7:18-19 *(NIV)*
1 Corinthians 15:21-22 *(NIV)*
Galatians 5:17 *(NIV)*
John 20:21-22 *(NIV)*
Acts 8:17 *(NIV)*
2 Timothy 1:6 *(NIV)*

Chapter 5 — The Human Condition: Life Under Compromised Code

Proverbs 16:25 *(NIV)*
Ecclesiastes 3:11 *(NIV)*
Isaiah 64:6 *(NIV)*
Matthew 23:27-28 *(NIV)*
John 4:13-14 *(NIV)*
Romans 7:15, 22-24 *(NIV)*

Chapter 6 — The Law: The Diagnostic That Could Not Heal

Genesis 6:5 *(NIV)*
Exodus 20:1-3 *(NIV)*
Exodus 20:17 *(NIV)*
Jeremiah 31:33 *(NIV)*
Matthew 5:20 *(NIV)*
Romans 2:14-15 *(NIV)*
Romans 3:20 *(NIV)*
Romans 7:7 *(NIV)*
Galatians 3:21 *(NIV)*
Galatians 3:22 *(NIV)*
Galatians 3:24-25 *(NIV)*
Hebrews 7:19 *(NIV)*
James 1:23-25 *(NIV)*

Chapter 7 — Written Within: Heart of Stone and Heart of Flesh

Jeremiah 31:31-34 *(NIV)*
Ezekiel 36:26-27 *(NIV)*
Ezekiel 36:26 *(NIV)*
Zechariah 7:12 *(NIV)*
2 Corinthians 3:3 *(NIV)*
2 Corinthians 5:17 *(NIV)*
Hebrews 8:10 *(NIV)*

Chapter 8 — Incompatibility: The Problem of a Holy God

Exodus 33:20 *(NIV)*
Isaiah 6:3 *(NIV)*
Isaiah 6:5 *(NIV)*
Isaiah 59:1-2 *(NIV)*
Habakkuk 1:13 *(NIV)*
Hebrews 9:7-8 *(NIV)*
Hebrews 12:14 *(NIV)*
John 3:3, 5-7 *(NIV)*

Chapter 9 — Rebirth: The Reinstallation of the Original Code

Genesis 2:7 *(NIV)*
Luke 1:35 *(NIV)*
Matthew 1:20 *(NIV)*
John 1:14 *(NIV)*
John 3:3 *(NIV)*
John 3:5-7 *(NIV)*
John 5:19 *(NIV)*
John 5:30 *(NIV)*
John 6:38 *(NIV)*
John 14:10 *(NIV)*
John 15:4-5 *(NIV)*
John 20:21-22 *(NIV)*
Romans 5:19 *(NIV)*
Romans 8:9-11 *(NIV)*
1 Corinthians 15:22 *(NIV)*
1 Corinthians 15:45-47 *(NIV)*
2 Corinthians 5:17 *(NIV)*
Galatians 2:20 *(NIV)*

Colossians 1:27 *(NIV)*
Titus 3:5 *(NIV)*
Hebrews 1:3 *(NIV)*
Hebrews 4:15 *(NIV)*
James 1:18 *(NIV)*
1 Peter 1:23 *(NIV)*

Chapter 10 — The Holy Spirit: The Override Signal

Matthew 7:20 *(NIV)*
John 14:16-17 *(NIV)*
John 16:8 *(NIV)*
John 16:13 *(NIV)*
Romans 6:13 *(NIV)*
Romans 8:14 *(NIV)*
Romans 12:1 *(NIV)*
Romans 12:2 *(NIV)*
2 Corinthians 7:10 *(NIV)*
Galatians 5:16 *(NIV)*
Galatians 5:17 *(NIV)*
Galatians 5:18 *(NIV)*
Galatians 5:22-23 *(NIV)*
Philippians 1:6 *(NIV)*

Chapter 11 — The Process: Transformation Over Time

Proverbs 24:16 *(NIV)*
Romans 8:29 *(NIV)*
2 Corinthians 3:18 *(NIV)*
Ephesians 4:22-24 *(NIV)*
Philippians 2:12-13 *(NIV)*
Philippians 3:12-14 *(NIV)*
Colossians 3:9-10 *(NIV)*
Hebrews 5:14 *(NIV)*
1 John 1:8-9 *(NIV)*

Chapter 12 — Three Layers of Restoration: Justified, Regenerated, Sanctified

Romans 3:23-24 *(NIV)*
Romans 5:1 *(NIV)*

Romans 8:1 *(NIV)*
Romans 8:30 *(NIV)*
1 Corinthians 6:11 *(NIV)*
2 Corinthians 5:17 *(NIV)*
1 Thessalonians 5:23 *(NIV)*
Titus 3:5 *(NIV)*
1 Peter 1:3 *(NIV)*

Chapter 13 — False Fixes: Why Nothing External Reaches the Source

Genesis 1:27 *(NIV)*
Ecclesiastes 2:10-11 *(NIV)*
Ecclesiastes 12:13 *(NIV)*
Jeremiah 2:13 *(NIV)*
Matthew 7:20 *(NIV)*
Matthew 11:28-30 *(NIV)*
Matthew 15:8-9 *(NIV)*
Matthew 16:26 *(NIV)*
John 15:5 *(NIV)*
Ephesians 2:1, 4-5 *(NIV)*
Philippians 3:19 *(NIV)*
Colossians 3:3 *(NIV)*
2 Timothy 3:5 *(NIV)*
Hebrews 11:25 *(NIV)*

Chapter 14 — Running Restored: Life in Alignment with the Source

Psalm 37:4 *(NIV)*
Ezekiel 36:26-27 *(NIV)*
Mark 1:41-42 *(NIV)*
Mark 12:30-31 *(NIV)*
Luke 10:17, 19-20 *(NIV)*
John 5:19 *(NIV)*
John 13:34-35 *(NIV)*
John 14:27 *(NIV)*
Romans 6:13 *(NIV)*
Romans 12:2 *(NIV)*
Romans 12:4-5 *(NIV)*
Romans 13:10 *(NIV)*
1 Corinthians 6:19-20 *(NIV)*
1 Corinthians 13:1-3 *(NIV)*
2 Corinthians 4:8-9 *(NIV)*

2 Corinthians 4:16-18 *(NIV)*
2 Corinthians 10:5 *(NIV)*
2 Corinthians 12:9 *(NIV)*
Ephesians 4:29 *(NIV)*
Philippians 3:12 *(NIV)*
Philippians 4:6-7 *(NIV)*
Philippians 4:8 *(NIV)*
Colossians 3:23-24 *(NIV)*
Hebrews 6:19 *(NIV)*
Hebrews 10:24-25 *(NIV)*
James 3:9-10 *(NIV)*
James 5:14-16 *(NIV)*
1 Peter 1:6-7 *(NIV)*
1 John 3:14 *(NIV)*
1 John 4:7-8 *(NIV)*
1 John 4:8 *(NIV)*
1 John 4:16 *(NIV)*

Chapter 15 — The Kingdom: The Restoration of All Things

Mark 1:15 *(NIV)*
Matthew 6:10 *(NIV)*
Romans 8:19-22 *(NIV)*
Romans 16:20 *(NIV)*
1 Corinthians 15:25-26 *(NIV)*
1 Corinthians 15:42-44 *(NIV)*
1 Corinthians 15:54-57 *(NIV)*
Philippians 3:20-21 *(NIV)*
Revelation 21:1-4 *(NIV)*
Revelation 21:3 *(NIV)*
Revelation 21:5 *(NIV)*
Revelation 21:22-23 *(NIV)*
Revelation 22:1-2 *(NIV)*
Revelation 22:3-4 *(NIV)*
Revelation 22:17 *(NIV)*
Revelation 22:20 *(NIV)*

For Further Study

Readers who wish to go deeper into the languages, history, and doctrine behind this book may find the following resources helpful. None of them is required to follow the argument; all of them have, in one way or another, shaped the mind of the author and of many who have taught him.

Biblical Languages and Lexicons

The Brown-Driver-Briggs Hebrew and English Lexicon (BDB), originally edited by Francis Brown, S. R. Driver, and Charles A. Briggs, remains a standard reference for Hebrew word study. The Hebrew and Aramaic Lexicon of the Old Testament (HALOT), edited by Ludwig Koehler and Walter Baumgartner, is the current scholarly standard. For New Testament Greek, A Greek-English Lexicon of the New Testament and Other Early Christian Literature (BDAG), edited by Frederick William Danker, is the standard academic lexicon. Strong's Exhaustive Concordance of the Bible, with its numbered system, remains a widely accessible entry point for lay readers seeking to study original-language terms.

The Doctrine of Sin, Grace, and Regeneration

Augustine of Hippo's Confessions and On the Trinity remain foundational for understanding inherited corruption and divine grace. John Calvin's Institutes of the Christian Religion is a sustained systematic treatment of the themes of this book. Jonathan Edwards's Religious Affections, John Owen's On the Mortification of Sin in Believers, and J. I. Packer's Knowing God are classic treatments of the interior life of the

Christian under grace. Anthony Hoekema's Created in God's Image and Saved by Grace are thorough modern treatments of biblical anthropology and soteriology.

The Kingdom of God and the New Creation

George Eldon Ladd's The Presence of the Future remains the classic evangelical treatment of inaugurated eschatology. N. T. Wright's Surprised by Hope and The Resurrection of the Son of God develop a robust theology of bodily resurrection and new creation. Herman Ridderbos's The Coming of the Kingdom and Geerhardus Vos's Biblical Theology are deeper reading for those who wish to follow the theme of the kingdom through the whole of Scripture.

By the Same Author

Cassius Stuart, Success, The Total Package — a complementary treatment of the positive, integrated shape of human life when achievement, relationships, character, purpose, and spirit are running together rather than at cross-purposes. Readers of the present book who wish to think further about what restored human life looks like in its practical outworking will find that earlier book a useful companion.

OTHER BOOKS BY
Dr. CASSIUS V. STUART

Success, The Total Package
English Version
979-8-218-16590-1

A New Start in Business
English Version
978-0-57849197-4

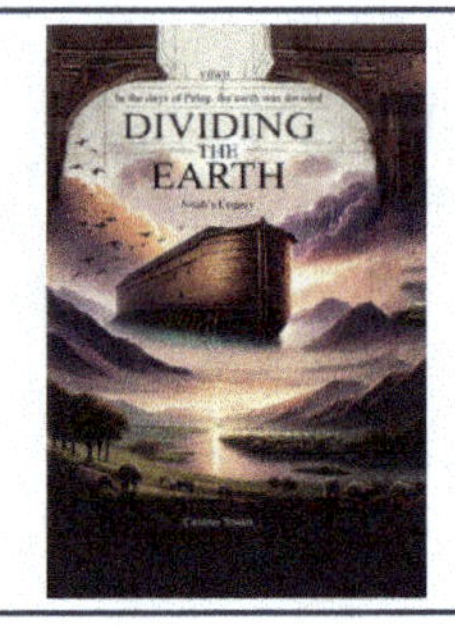

Dividing the Earth
English Version
979-8-9896368-0-8

Syiera, The Dragon Slayer
English Version
979-8-9896368-1-5

Raquell: A Tale of Magic & Might
English Version
979-8-9896368-2-2

The Longest 30 Days
English Version
979-8-9896368-4-6

FORTHCOMING BOOKS BY Dr. CASSIUS V. STUART

When the Freedom Fighters Become the Slave Masters
English Version
ISBN 979-8-9896368-5-3

From Can't See to Can't See
English Version
ISBN 979-8-9896368-7-7

The Zero Paradigm
English Version
ISBN 979-8-9958941-2-4

Reflections
English Version
ISBN 979-8-9958941-0-0

The Political Cost of Broken Trust
English Version
ISBN 979-8-9896368-9-1

The Hidden Frequency
English Version
ISBN 979-8-9958941-3-1

www.ingramcontent.com/pod-product-compliance
Lightning Source LLC
LaVergne TN
LVHW010552110826
845149LV00003B/637

* 9 7 9 8 9 9 5 8 9 4 1 1 7 *